D0273159

331.137 8462.09
CON

Ce

Unemployment
in Britain between
the Wars

HILLCROFT COLLEGE
LIBRARY
SOUTH BANK
SURBITON
SURREY KT6 6DF

36 846

SEMINAR STUDIES IN HISTORY

A full list of titles in this series will be found on the back cover of this book.

SEMINAR STUDIES IN HISTORY

Editor: Patrick Richardson

Unemployment in Britain between the Wars

Stephen Constantine

Lecturer in History,
University of Lancaster

LONGMAN

LONGMAN GROUP LIMITED

Longman House
Burnt Mill, Harlow, Essex CM20 2JE, England
and Associated Companies throughout the World.

© Longman Group Ltd. 1980

*All rights reserved. No part of this publication may
be reproduced, stored in a retrieval system, or
transmitted in any form or by any means, electronic,
mechanical, photocopying, recording, or otherwise, without
the prior written permission of the Publishers.*

First published 1980
Third impression 1985

ISBN 0 582 35232 0

Set in 10/11 Press Roman, IBM

Produced by Longman Group (F.E.) Ltd.
Printed in Hong Kong

British Library Cataloguing in Publication Data

Constantine, Stephen
  Unemployment in Britain between the Wars. —
  (Seminar studies in history).
  1. Labour supply — Great Britain — History
  — 20th century
  I. Title II. Series
  331.1'37941   HD5765.A6

ISBN 0-582-35232-0

Contents

Introduction to the Series

The seminar method of teaching is being used increasingly. It is a way of learning in smaller groups through discussion, designed both to get away from and to supplement the basic lecture techniques. To be successful, the members of a seminar must be informed — or else, in the unkind phrase of a cynic — it can be a 'pooling of ignorance'. The chapter in the textbook of English or European history by its nature cannot provide material in this depth, but at the same time the full academic work may be too long and perhaps too advanced.

For this reason we have invited practising teachers to contribute short studies on specialised aspects of British and European history with these special needs in mind. For this series the authors have been asked to provide, in addition to their basic analysis, a full selection of documentary material of all kinds and an up-to-date and comprehensive bibliography. Both these sections are referred to in the text, but it is hoped that they will prove to be valuable teaching and learning aids in themselves.

Note on the System of References:
A bold number in round brackets (5) in the text refers the reader to the corresponding entry in the Bibliography section at the end of the book. A bold number in square brackets, preceded by 'doc' [docs 6, 8] refers the reader to the corresponding items in the section of Documents, which follows the main text.

PATRICK RICHARDSON
General Editor

Acknowledgements

In preparing my text I received much help and valued criticism from two of my colleagues, Dr Eric Evans and Dr Gordon Phillips. I am grateful for their assistance. I also wish to record my sincere thanks for the admirable secretarial support I have received from Miss Linda Parkinson and from Wendy, my wife.

Stephen Constantine

We are grateful to the following for permission to reproduce copyright material: The Rt. Hon. Julian Amery, M.P. for an extract from a letter by L.S. Amery to Stanley Baldwin dated 11th Feb. 1924 from the *Amery Papers Box G.82;* H.L. Beales for extracts from *Memoirs of the Unemployed* edited by H.L. Beales and R.S. Lambert, pub. by Victor Gollancz Ltd; The Controller of Her Majesty's Stationery Office for data from *Investigation in the Coalfields of South Wales — Cmd.3272* and *Third Report of the Commissioner for the Special Areas — Cmd. 5303;* James Nisbet & Co. Ltd for extracts from *The Unemployed Man* by E.W. Bakke.

The Strube cartoon on the cover appeared in the Daily Express in 1936 and is reproduced by permission of London Express News and Feature Services.

Part One: The Background

1 The Unemployment Problem

For many years historians have been struggling to modify a deeply entrenched view which regards the interwar period, and especially the 1930s, as essentially a time of persistent depression, gloom and failure. In contrast they have properly emphasized the real achievements of these two decades. Far from being uniformly years of suffering, there was much that justified celebration. Greatly helped by a fall in the cost of living in the 1920s and early 1930s, average real wage earnings between the wars went up, until by 1938 they were perhaps one-third higher than in 1913 (2). The expansion of the chemical, motor car, electrical and other consumer goods industries and of the retailing trade provided better-paid jobs for more workers. Moreover, parents were limiting the size of their families and with fewer mouths to feed incomes went further. On average, hours of work were also down. As a result more and more people were left with higher real earnings and greater leisure.

The consequence was a conspicuous improvement in the living standards of the majority of people in Britain. For some it brought real affluence, perhaps the opportunity to own a sparkling mass-produced motor car, an Austin or a Morris, or a chance to buy a semi-detached house with a garden and modern conveniences in one of the new estates being laid out in the suburbs. For many more people it meant at least some additional domestic comforts. Better equipped, newly built council houses were available for rent; modern furniture, radios, labour-saving household equipment such as electric cookers and other consumer goods could be bought. There was more cash left over for entertainments. Audiences packed the cinemas and dance halls with regular enthusiasm, and more people were taking annual holidays, many in the holiday camps which sprang up on the coast in places like Skegness and Pwllheli. Most strikingly, social investigators found a marked drop in the number of people condemned to live in poverty. Dire need still regrettably existed, but it was much less prominent between the wars than it had been in the supposedly golden days of Edwardian England.

Another valuable result of higher incomes was an increase in the consumption of better food: more vegetables, fruit and dairy products for example. Together with improved medical and social services, this brought about an impressive advance in the health of the nation as a whole. Death rates fell, life expectancy increased. The killer diseases of the nineteenth century such as tuberculosis, typhoid, scarlet fever and diphtheria were in retreat by 1939. These were years of progress when, in spite of the depression, economic growth was above prewar levels and material living standards improved (2, 7, 8, 11, 28).

And yet these realities have on the whole failed to prevent a bitter and gloomy image of the interwar years from surviving to this day. These years are still characterised as a period of mass unemployment when, particularly in the North and in Wales, once prosperous industries and the workers who served them were suffering. There remain sharp pictures of out-of-work men clustered at dusty street corners, and of the abandoned shipyards at Jarrow on the Tyne [doc. 1]. Nor, as this study is intended to show, are these impressions entirely misleading. Unemployment did blight the lives of many people, and the issue became an unavoidable topic of public discussion and an inescapable worry for government ministers. Interwar Britain was, then, a land of contrasts [doc. 2]. Indeed, set against the average rise in living standards and the prosperous regions of the country, the wasted years of the unemployed and the decay of the depressed areas stand out more starkly. Unemployment was as much a feature of the 1920s and 1930s as busy new factories, modern housing estates and cinemas built like fantasy palaces.

The problem of unemployment was not new to British society. It had been a recurrent blight in the nineteenth and early twentieth centuries, and the bitterness and distress it caused lay behind many of the social and political disturbances of those years. What was unprecedented about the interwar unemployment problem was its extent, its duration and its effects.

Attempts to compare the extent of unemployment between the wars with the level before 1914 are hampered by the absence of satisfactory statistics, particularly for the earlier period (18). Not until the 1920 Unemployment Insurance Act began to operate were reasonably accurate figures made available. Except for domestic servants, agricultural labourers and civil servants, this Act provided unemployment insurance cover for most manual workers and other employees earning less than £250 a year (67). Henceforth it was possible to calculate the number of insured people out of work and the rate of unemployment (expressed as a percentage of the insured labour force). Before the war we have to rely on figures which are far less comprehensive but which give us some idea of the extent of unemployment among that small proportion of the workforce organised in trade unions. The figures therefore tend to cover mainly skilled and semi-skilled workers. What they show is that in the period 1881 to 1913 unemployment among these workers in the United Kingdom was on average about 4.8 per cent (expressed as a percentage of trade unionists). The rate fluctuated a good deal but at its maximum in 1886 it was about 10 per cent **(17)**.

In spite of the inadequacies of these figures for comparative purposes it is probably true that the extent of unemployment was seriously higher between the wars. Following a short sharp economic boom in 1919–20, depression settled like a dark cloud over the United Kingdom. There were fluctuations in the density of this cloud but it never lifted before the outbreak of the Second World War. Between 1921 and 1939 unemployment averaged 14 per cent of the insured workforce. Records show an early peak of 16.9 per cent in 1921 and a later one of 22.1 per cent in 1932. Once the depression began there were never less than one million workers out of a job. There were over two million insured workers registered as unemployed in December 1921, and in January 1933, the worst month of all, there were 2,979,000 **(17, 19)**. If we add those unemployed workers who for one reason or another did not register as unemployed we reach an estimated total of 3,750,000 in September 1932. Taking into account the families of the unemployed, six or seven million people in the United Kingdom were living on the dole in the worst months of the depression in the early 1930s **(12)**.

What made unemployment such a scourge between the wars was not just its extent but also its duration. In the thirty years or so before 1914 workers might be hit by a run of three or four years of high unemployment. In the bad years 1884–7 unemployment remained over 7 per cent. There were other periods – 1892–5, 1903–5, 1908–10 – when unemployment climbed to over 5 or 6 per cent. But between these clusters of grim years there were times of improved trade and better employment prospects when rates of unemployment fell to 2 or 3 per cent. In the 1920s and 1930s, however, the depression seemed to be far less a temporary dislocation. Only in 1927 did the rate of unemployment slip temporarily below 10 per cent. Unemployment remained a permanent burden in British society between the wars **(17, 19)**.

The effect on the individual worker might be serious. For most people a period of unemployment was usually short. In September 1929 nearly 90 per cent of those who applied for unemployment benefits and allowances in Britain had been unemployed for less than six months. But since a surprisingly large number of insured workers changed jobs at least once a year, with consistently high levels of unemployment the chances of repeated bouts of unemployment between

3

jobs were higher and the effect of these on savings, living standards and morale could be grave. Moreover, the tendency for workers to suffer from long-term unemployment, lasting for twelve months or more, eventually developed as one of the most worrying features of the 1930s. In September 1929 less than 5 per cent of those applying for unemployment relief in Britain, about 45,000, had been unemployed for twelve months or more, but by August 1932, near the bottom of the depression, there were over 400,000, making 16.4 per cent of the total. Such recovery as then took place left many of these workers still without a job: the long-term unemployed numbered over 330,000 and formed 25 per cent of the total number of unemployed workers in August 1936. As late as August 1939 there were 244,000 long-term unemployed, nearly 23 per cent of the total. For many workers in the 1930s there was little prospect of ever finding a job again (17, 50).

Even before 1914 unemployment had become a public issue. Economists and social scientists had begun to examine more seriously the causes of industrial unemployment and had identified some of its social consequences. The labour movement had helped make the provision of work and the relief of distress a political issue. Politicians of all parties had offered panaceas of varying degrees of value, and there had been some government action (60, 65). But the severity of the interwar depression had more far-reaching consequences. Unemployment reflected fundamental changes in the nation's economic structure. It affected living standards and the quality of life for many workers in Britain. It aroused considerable concern about the damage it was doing to the physical and mental wellbeing of its victims. It forced a major re-examination of many well-established ideas and assumptions about the role of the state as an economic manager and as a provider of welfare services. And it profoundly altered the demands and expectations of the British people. To a considerable extent, the failures of interwar Britain rather than the real achievements had the greater effect on government policy and popular aspirations.

2 Economic Causes

Total national figures of the number of unemployed workers in the United Kingdom in each year disguise the variety of problems which account for unemployment. Before the First World War and especially between the wars social scientists began to classify the types of unemployment which together accounted for high national totals. They defined them as personal, frictional, seasonal, cyclical and structural unemployment. It is not easy to distinguish the predominant factor in the case of each individual worker, and one cause of unemployment undoubtedly affected the severity of others. But the concepts involved do help clarify the economic problems from which Britain suffered between the wars.

To begin with there were those unfortunate people who were unemployed primarily for personal reasons; because of physical or mental handicaps they were only marginally members of the labour force. Most of them were not unemployable, for in times of economic boom their services might be required, but in normal years, and especially in times of depression, they were often the first people to be laid off and the last to be re-employed. Quite a lot of the long-term unemployed, out of work for twelve months or more, were found to be suffering from some form of disability in the 1930s although few of them were incapable of any work (50).

Frictional unemployment tended to be short-term. In any year, irrespective of economic boom and slump and for a variety of reasons, thousands of workers changed jobs. Many of them found new employment fairly rapidly, but while looking for new openings they usually registered temporarily as unemployed. In addition a number of workers such as dock workers were employed only on a casual basis and might find themselves without work for two or three working days each week. Seasonal unemployment was also normally short-term. Even in an industrial society activity in certain trades varied with the time of year. Building workers, for example, often found themselves unemployed in winter. Total unemployment figures were therefore usually higher in the winter months than in the summer.

5

Cyclical unemployment

Between the wars people were much more concerned with cyclical unemployment. This not only affected more workers but might leave them without a job for many months. During the nineteenth century businessmen had been aware of a fairly regular cycle of economic boom followed by economic slump. In periods of boom British exports overseas rose, investment in new factories at home increased, industrial output went up, wages might rise and the labour force was fully employed. But then followed the downturn. The value of exports fell, investment slackened off, output dropped and wages might fall. The only thing that rose was cyclical unemployment. Peaks of higher unemployment and social distress were repeated at intervals of about eight to ten years. Explanations of the trade cycle are complex, but one thing is clear. The British business cycle was not due to factors operating solely within Britain. From the last quarter of the nineteenth century the pattern of boom closely followed fluctuations in the business activity of other nations overseas, especially France, Germany and the United States. Because of the type of economic structure that had evolved in Britain by the end of the century, the level of prosperity at home had become crucially susceptible to booms and slumps overseas.

By 1914 Britain had such a specialised industrial economy that she needed to import over half of her food supplies and about seven-eighths of the raw materials needed by industry. To pay for these imports she relied mostly on the sale of her own products abroad. In the decade before the First World War the output of more than one British worker in every four was exported (14). Moreover those exports were made up of a limited range of products: 38 per cent were textiles, mainly cotton goods, 14 per cent iron and steel, 10 per cent coal and 10 per cent engineering products including ships (9, 10). These were the staple export industries, relying heavily on their overseas sales. Early in the century about 33 per cent of the coal mined in Britain, 22 per cent of the ships built, 79 per cent of the cotton goods manufactured and 50 per cent of the iron and steel produced were exported (2, 6). Inevitably a slump in the United States, in Europe or elsewhere reduced demand in those markets for these products and seriously affected Britain's prosperity. Since the cotton, coal, shipbuilding and iron and steel industries together employed about two million workers before the First World War, a downturn in the business cycle overseas had a profound effect on the level of employment in Britain. Moreover repercussions were felt in other industries as a result. Depression and unemployment in the staple export industries reduced incomes at home and hence the demand for the products of other British industries catering more for the home market. Consequently depression in overseas markets spread via depression in Britain's export industries to other sectors of the economy and unemployment became more widespread.

In the years between the wars this prewar trade cycle continued to operate. As before, the fairly regular pattern of boom and slump was repeated. Once again the staple export industries were sensitive to fluctuations in levels of demand overseas. Once again depression in those industries was transmitted to other sectors of the domestic economy. The alarming new features of the cycle in these years were the severity of the depressions and the limited extent of the subsequent recoveries.

Initially, wartime expectations that Britain would enjoy unprecedented prosperity after the war seemed to be realised. During 1919—20 exports rose and much new investment took place, especially in the cotton and shipbuilding industries. Wages rose and unemployment fell. But then came a downturn of unexpected severity. In 1921 the volume of exports from the United Kingdom fell to 50 per cent of the level of 1913; industrial production slumped, money wages fell and unemployment rose to the disturbing peak of nearly 17 per cent. Economic dislocation and currency instability delayed economic recovery in Europe but by the mid-1920s improvements there and especially expansion in the United States increased overseas demand for British exports. However, even in 1929 they reached only 80 per cent of the volume of 1913. Other industries producing consumer goods for the home market grew a little and there was an upturn in building activity. But recovery was slow compared to the United States and with unemployment still high it hardly seemed complete before a new downturn began in 1929.

The world depression of 1929—32 which followed seemed to many observers to herald the final collapse of capitalism. There were two features of the slump overseas which were bound to create more cyclical unemployment in Britain. The bursting of the Wall Street stock market boom in 1929 devastated business confidence in America, reduced the level of her domestic investment, cut real income by 37 per cent and pushed her unemployment rates over 30 per cent. As a result American consumption fell, and with it went the demand for British products. Britain's staple export trades were hit. This American depression caused parallel depressions in other industrial countries in Europe, reducing their demand for British products. It also exacerbated the problems of the non-industrialised nations, and this was the second feature of the overseas slump which hit Britain. Even before the American collapse, the prices of food and raw materials exported by those countries had begun to fall. A devastated American and European economy then demanded less of those products and their prices fell even more. Earning less abroad, those countries could afford to buy fewer industrial products; as a major supplier of such products Britain suffered.

Together these two features of the slump overseas shattered British exporters once again: in 1931 and 1932 exports were about half the volume of 1913. Depression in that sector of the economy on such a scale inevitably reduced total domestic consumption and therefore depressed investment, output and employment in many other industries. Total unemployment reached a new level of over 22 per cent in 1932. The revival which then took place was more rapid than in the United States but, significantly, it was led by industries which catered more for the domestic market. Exports were slower to recover. Just before the Second World War the proportion of production going to export was one in eight, half the level of before 1914. And the recovery, which reached a peak in 1937, still left much unused industrial capacity and high unemployment (2, 14).

The business cycle goes a long way towards explaining variations in the rate of unemployment. During periods of recovery and boom the rates fell; when depression struck they rose. In those bad years, unemployment was severe and widespread. An enquiry undertaken in August 1922 showed high rates of unemployment for workers in some of the staple export industries: 39 per cent in shipbuilding and 24 per cent in engineering and the metal industries. The coal industry was not yet affected by depression and cotton industry employees tended to be on short time rather than out of work. In other industries affected by this cyclical downturn unemployment was serious. High rates were recorded in the pottery, glass, chemical and brick industries, in the building trade and among dockers, seamen and transport workers (30). When cyclical depression struck again in 1929–32, high and even more widespread unemployment was experienced. In 1932 the staple export industries were all very distressed with high unemployment rates: 35 per cent of coalminers, about 46 per cent of iron and steel workers, 62 per cent of shipbuilders and repairers, 31 per cent of cotton workers. But as before, unemployment troubled many other trades as well. For example, 36 per cent of workers in the potteries were out of a job (19).

These cyclical depressions clearly created much distress, and victims of cyclical unemployment from many trades trooped down to the labour exchanges to join the queues. According to orthodox economic theory at the time, their plight would only be temporary, since economic boom would inevitably follow depression. It is true that a recovery took place later in the 1920s and again in the 1930s, and many workers found jobs. But the striking feature of these years is that even at the height of the booms, in 1929 and in 1937, there were still high levels of unemployment, much of it long-term, especially concentrated in the staple export trades. In 1929 there was still a 19 per cent rate among coal miners, about 17 per cent among iron and steel workers, 25 per cent among shipbuilders and repairers, 13 per cent among cotton workers. Similarly in 1937 the rates were 16 per cent for coalminers, about 11 per cent for iron and steel workers, 24 per cent for shipbuilders and repairers, 11 per cent for cotton workers. Generally, other industries which had been afflicted at the bottom of the depressions had recovered much better during the booms (19).

These figures reveal that cyclical unemployment was not the only cause of high rates of unemployment between the wars. At the height of economic recovery cyclical unemployment would be relieved and unemployment rates should have dropped to the 2 or 3 per cent levels experienced in booms before the First World War. This did not happen. Instead unemployment rates levelled out in years of recovery (1929 and 1937) at rates rather similar to those recorded in the worst years of depression before the war. What this suggests is that there had been a permanent fall in the demand for certain industrial products over and above that created by cyclical fluctuations. Such a change revealed weaknesses in the structure of the British economy, caused drastic contractions in the demand for labour in certain industries, and therefore produced structural unemployment.

Structural unemployment

The industries which faced this permanent decline in demand for their products were coal, cotton, shipbuilding and, to a lesser extent, iron and steel. They were the great growth industries of the nineteenth century, the sectors which dominated exports before 1914 and which had made Britain for a time the workshop of the world. In 1913 the peak output of the coal industry in the United Kingdom was achieved: 287 million tons. Even in the best years between the wars, production was about 60 million tons lower. Cotton production similarly fell, the output of cloth in the boom year 1937 being nearly half the quantity made in 1912. Before the First World War British shipyards had dominated the world, but this was never the case between the wars and the tonnage of ships built was generally much less. The iron and steel industry had a chequered experience. Total output did increase and a permanent decline in the industry was avoided, but this was largely due to a slow expansion of steel production which balanced a fall in pig-iron production. The problem in the iron and steel industry was the existence of excess unused capacity. Inadequate demand for products left equipment, and labour, unemployed. If excess capacity troubled an industry which actually expanded total output, the extent of that problem in the declining coal, cotton and shipbuilding industries may be imagined. It was especially unfortunate that during the war and in the short postwar boom heavy investment in iron and steel plants, shipyards and cotton factories had boosted capacity above prewar levels. Much of that investment had been made on the assumption that demand would increase in the future. In fact demand stagnated or actually fell (2, 9, 10).

In part, reduced demand for British products reflected changing consumer needs and tastes at home and overseas. World consumption of coal grew at a much lower rate after the war than before, partly due to more efficient uses of fuel in homes and by industry and partly because of changes to alternative sources of power: oil, gas and, principally, electricity. Whereas the world's prewar mercantile marine consisted of steamships using coal, by 1939 over half these fleets were oil-powered. Similarly, traditional cotton textiles had to compete with new man-made fibres like rayon, while a notorious 1920s revolution in women's fashions raised eyebrows but lowered demand for cloth. Technical progress had improved the speed and carrying capacity of shipping and therefore fewer ships were required, and in any case the decline in world trade in the 1930s discouraged companies from ordering new vessels. As already mentioned, demand for pig-iron fell when more use was made of steel (2). These changes in world demand inevitably affected an economy heavily committed to producing such products.

Demand for British products was also disturbed by the emergence of serious competition from producers overseas. This challenge from the United States, Western Europe and Japan was discernible even before the First World War. In 1850 Britain's share of total world industrial output was about 30 per cent. Already by 1910 it had shrunk to 13 per cent. Newly industrialised nations almost inevitably produced the relatively simple commodities which formed Britain's staple exports. Manufacturing for themselves they had less need for British products. Long before 1914 British exporters had found rapidly expanding markets only in the more distant non-industrialised regions of America, Asia and Africa. The First World War accelerated these ominous developments. When the British economy was concentrating on the production of essential war materials, overseas customers could not be so easily supplied. Overseas industrialists facing less competition from

Britain expanded their production. After the war more mature and efficient rivals had emerged. By 1930 Britain's share of total world industrial output had declined still further to 10.5 per cent (5). Competition was particularly felt in the staple export industries. Shortages of British coal exports during the war had encouraged the opening or expansion of mines in Germany, Poland, the Netherlands, Spain and the Far East. Major textile industries grew during the war in Japan and India, important British markets before 1914. Rival shipyards had opened in the United States, Japan, Holland and Scandinavia. World iron and steel-making capacity also expanded during the war, especially in the United States, and challenged British companies later (2, 9, 12).

With such increases in the world's capacity to produce staple industrial products, competition between the wars was bound to be fierce. Price, quality and speed of delivery were not, however, to be the sole determining factors in such a struggle. The most serious additional factor was government interference in the market. The international free trade world had worked to Britain's advantage in the nineteenth century, but it was being eroded towards the close. The interwar years then saw the imposition of even higher tariff barriers by foreign governments, especially in the 1930s, to preserve their home markets for their own producers. Currency devaluations and exchange controls additionally undermined free competition. Many foreign governments subsidised their own shipbuilders to help them compete for foreign orders. In the struggle for national economic self-sufficiency world trade was inevitably choked and an economy like Britain's, heavily committed to exports, suffered in consequence. The sort of retaliatory measures taken by the British government, such as the introduction of tariffs, could do little to undo the damage.

It was not, however, true that the problems of the staple industries were entirely due to factors outside British control. War and postwar inflation and wage rises had increased the comparative costs of British products. Government policy, particularly the return to the gold standard at the prewar parity in 1925, possibly compounded the problem and left British goods overpriced on international markets. But more serious was the inefficiency of many British firms. This may be a factor explaining declining British coal exports between the wars. Especially in the 1920s there were many small companies in operation without the resources to invest in more efficient methods of production and distribution. Output per man was down on prewar rates in the 1920s and picked up only with the spread of mechanisation in the 1930s. It remained for the most part a high-cost industry at a time when static world demand and expanding world production led to fierce competition. The inefficiency of the cotton industry is even more apparent. The industry had been slow to convert to ring-spinning, automatic looms and electric power before the war, and the severity of falling sales between the wars discouraged new investment in more efficient techniques. British shipyards were also tending to become obsolete. Technical advances were slow to spread and the industry was backward in switching from steam to diesel engines. Reorganisation and new investment was difficult to carry out when demand was low. Similarly the iron and steel industry remained a high cost producer, slow to adopt new techniques and to shift from acid to basic steel production in response to changes in world requirements (2, 9, 12).

Thus handicapped, it is not surprising that these industries could not overcome the adverse trading conditions and stiff competition of the interwar years. Products were squeezed out of the home markets of rival producers, and struggled to compete with the export drives of those rivals in non-industrialised markets. The prewar European market for British goods had been large though slow-growing; it declined between the wars. The United States had been a huge if static market before 1914 but sales dropped sharply in the 1930s. The markets of South and Central America and Asia (including India) had been growing rapidly until the war but they withered after it. Only the Africa market expanded consistently from small prewar beginnings. British salesmen were forced to retreat into the more sympathetic markets of the Empire, but this could not halt the decline in the volume of British overseas trade (14, 63).

This decline was exposed in the export figures of the large staple industries. Apart from 1923 when the French occupation of the Ruhr caused the closure of German coal mines and a remarkable boost to British coal exports, sales were well down on prewar levels. Similarly there were savage reductions in cotton exports from just under 7,000 million square yards in 1913 to under 3,800 million square yards in 1929 and to 2,000 million square yards even at the peak of the next trade cycle in 1937. The decline then continued. While at the end of the 1920s shipbuilding orders from overseas rose slightly above prewar levels, they dropped badly in the 1930s. Iron and steel exports did reasonably well in the late 1920s but after the disasters of the early 1930s recovery was slight. In the best year, 1937, exports were barely over half prewar levels (2, 9, 10) [docs 3, 4].

Such figures give some indication of the squeezing out of British products from overseas markets which they had previously dominated. It was even more galling, and additional proof of the lack of competitiveness of some British industries, that even the home market was being invaded by foreign products. In the past British manufacturers had for the most part launched exports from the secure platform of a monopoly of their home market. Between the wars, mainly because of lower costs, higher efficiency or government subsidies, foreign manufacturers began to challenge home producers. The coal industry did not suffer this embarrassment, but Lancashire shuddered when nineteenth century trade patterns were ironically reversed and India began to export cotton goods to Britain. Japanese products were to follow. British shipping companies were buying vessels overseas: in 1936 imports totalled nearly 15 per cent of the tonnage delivered to British owners, and in that year imports exceeded exports. Imports of iron and steel also rose sharply in the later years of the 1920s. This invasion was checked in the 1930s only when the British government gave in to the repeated demands of the Iron and Steel Federation and imposed heavy duties on imports (2, 7, 9, 10).

It was clear that Britain was no longer the workshop of the world. A relative decline in Britain's predominance was inevitable once other nations industrialised. This erosion had been taking place since the last quarter of the nineteenth century. But the stagnation or absolute decline in output and exports by the big staple industries of the country are an indication of more profound changes. Partly they suggest the lack of competitiveness of British products. But largely they reflect the structural imbalance in the economy. Britain's heavy commitment to the production of coal, cotton goods, ships and iron and steel was bound to cause problems when the world's capacity to produce these goods had increased and greatly exceeded demand. Britain's investing of more and more capital in these industries before, during and immediately after the First World War may have seemed sensible by short-term calculations. But the need to diversify the economy, to shift resources into new industries, was in retrospect apparent. The consequences of overcommitment were the economic difficulties of the staple industries between the wars and the tragedy of large-scale structural unemployment. Overwhelmingly the dole queues were peopled by miners, cotton operatives, shipbuilders and iron and steel workers [doc. 6].

The plight of the workers was in a very real sense more serious than the troubles of the economy. In some respects even the battered staple industries had a good record. Although by international comparisons they remained for the most part uncompetitive, attempts were made to increase efficiency through the twenty years of the depression. The annual rate of growth of output per man between 1920 and 1938 was 2.5 per cent in mining, 1.6 per cent in textiles, 1.9 per cent in shipbuilding and 3.5 per cent in iron and steel. With the exception of this last, these performances were below the 2.8 per cent average of all industries but productivity was improving. Coal output per man went up largely because of more mechanisation. There were other, if smaller, technical advances in the cotton industry and in shipbuilding and some important innovations in iron and steel industry equipment (2, 9, 10). The improvements in these industries were not sufficient to enable them to regain lost ground in international markets, but productivity improvements do contrast favourably with the total output records of these industries which either stagnated or fell between 1920 and 1938. The apparent contradiction between increases in productivity and stagnant or declining industrial output is explained by serious reductions in the workforce of these industries.

It is this factor which justifies emphasis on the special plight of victims of structural unemployment. Percentage rates of unemployment for the staple industries disguise the fact that many workers had in addition been driven out of their accustomed trades entirely and were no longer classified as miners, cotton operatives, shipbuilders or iron and steel workers. They sought employment in other industries. Labour reductions were in part the consequence of those technical improvements which increased productivity; without significantly increasing total output fewer workers were required. But many workers were shed, especially in the 1930s, when deliberate attempts were made by employers' organisations to cut out surplus capacity and therefore reduce competition and maintain or raise prices. The number of coal mines operating was reduced and production concentrated in larger pits. Rationalisation schemes were organised by the Lancashire Cotton Corporation from 1929 and the Spindles Board, set up by government legislation in 1936, bought up and scrapped surplus spindles in the spinning section. The number of looms was also reduced. A similar process in the shipbuilding industry had by 1937 put out of operation twenty-eight shipyards with a total capacity of over one million tons [doc. 24]. Similarly, excess capacity in the steel industry was eliminated and plant reallocated around the country. These management decisions caused massive redundancies. A reduction in the size of the staple industries was a necessary part of the restructuring of the economy. But the process was painful because the labour dislodged was only partially absorbed by other industries (2, 12).

Much attention has been rightly devoted in recent years to the considerable total growth of the British economy between the wars, especially in the 1930s. Gross domestic product per head in the United Kingdom grew at an average of 1.8 per cent per annum between 1924 and 1937. This is better than the 1.1 per cent of 1855–1900 and the 0.7 per cent of 1900–14. Growth rates between the wars in Britain compared well internationally: the United States registered an average of 1.7 per cent between 1921 and 1937, Germany 2.2 per cent from 1928 to 1937 and France recorded an actual decline of 0.3 per cent between 1924 and 1937. Britain's growth partly reflected the productivity improvements in the staple industries but mainly the boom in building in the 1930s, and the expansion of new electrical engineering, motor-car, chemical and consumer goods industries catering for a home market which, mainly outside the depressed areas, showed many signs of prosperity (3, 7). But the expansion was often in capital intensive industries which employed comparatively little labour or which were insufficiently large to absorb more than a proportion of the labour which structural unemployment had made available. Indeed, one observed effect of structural unemployment was the drift of labour into other industries and the creation of pools of unemployment around them. Industries which had high rates of growth could not soak them up even in the middle of a boom year like 1937. At that time there were over 17,000 car workers unemployed, 15,000 workers from the chemical industry, 16,000 gas, water and electricity workers, 114,000 transport workers, 165,000 from the distributive trades. Unemployment in the building industry was high throughout the interwar years, largely because much unskilled labour was required and so entry into the industry was easy (17, 19). Structural unemployment caused by the problems of the depressed staple industries therefore damaged employment prospects in other trades.

This is one reason why accurate segregation and quantification of the types of unemployment is not possible. Calculations vary and what follows are rough estimates. It seems reasonable to suppose that personal, seasonal and frictional unemployment accounted for about 2 per cent of interwar unemployment rates. This was about the average level of unemployment in the 1950s and 1960s when cyclical and structural problems had been mainly overcome. In those years personal, seasonal and frictional unemployment remained, as between the wars, close to an irreducible minimum. At the height of the interwar booms, when cyclical unemployment must have been eliminated, total unemployment rates of around 10 per cent were recorded. Allowing for personal, frictional and seasonal unemployment this suggests a figure of about 8 per cent for structural unemployment, much of it by the 1930s of a serious long-term character. On top there rested in most years fluctuating figures for cyclical unemployment reaching about 7 per cent in the depression of 1921 and about 12 per cent in

Part Two: The Effects of Economic Depression

3 Social Consequences

One indication of the severity of the interwar economic depression is the number of contemporary investigations of the unemployment problem that it provoked. Government departments and official commissions investigated the extent of unemployment, examined the working of the unemployment insurance scheme and studied the effect of unemployment on the health of its victims. But often more useful to the historian were the investigations carried out by private individuals or organisations. To a remarkable extent the depressed areas remained unknown to many of the British people. But especially in the 1930s they were regions from which distressing reports emanated and to which writers, journalists and social scientists travelled, often with something of the self-conscious bravery of African explorers. Was the economic depression causing a major social disaster? Which places in Britain suffered most and what effect did unemployment have on the community? Who were the principal victims and how did it affect their living standards and health? Was the impact severe enough to undermine established patterns of working-class behaviour? Were families being broken up, was there a collapse of law and order and was the depression generating political militancy? How effectively were government policies and voluntary services meeting the needs of the unemployed? These were questions contemporaries often asked.

The geography of unemployment and migration

In the 1920s and 1930s the threat of unemployment hung over most workers in Britain irrespective of where they lived. Unemployment was a problem in seemingly the most unlikely places. When J.B. Priestley toured England in the autumn of 1933 he saw a crowd of unemployed workers around the labour exchange even in a small cathedral town like Salisbury (51). In the same year the Llandudno Advertiser recorded the formation of an Unemployed Welfare Committee [doc. 17]. Personal misfortune, individual decisions to change jobs and small local industrial changes created unemployment everywhere. More seriously, cyclical depressions affected most areas of the country. In August

1922 near the bottom of the slump unemployment was highest in Northern Ireland (25%) and in Scotland (21%). But it was also well above prewar averages in the North West (16%), North East (18%), Midlands (18%), South West (15%), South East (12%), London (13%) and Wales (12%) (**30**). Again, at the bottom of the severe depression in 1932 the annual rate was high in all regions, ranging from 13.5% in London to 36.5% in Wales (**17**). Few jobs were secure when overseas and home demand fell so far and workers were laid off in a wide range of industries. Even in the most prosperous regions at the most prosperous times unemployment remained abnormally high, swollen in part by the migration of the unemployed workers from the more depressed regions and industries. In 1936 when the Pilgrim Trust began its detailed study of unemployment in Britain it selected for examination the towns of Deptford, Leicester, Crook (Co. Durham), Blackburn, Liverpool and Rhondda (**50**). Unemployment was a blight on all areas of Britain.

Nevertheless vulnerability to unemployment and the severity of its effect depended a good deal on the industrial character of the area in which a worker lived. The regional distribution of industries created a regional pattern of unemployment. It was a pattern most starkly revealed at the peaks of industrial recovery. In 1929 the Ministry of Labour recorded unemployment rates above the national average in the North East (13.7%), North West (13.3%), Scotland (12.1%), and Wales (19.3%). Below the average were the Midlands (9.3%), South West (8.1%), South East (5.6%) and London (5.6%). The division was exactly repeated in 1937 with high rates in the North East (11%), North West (14%), North (17.9%), Scotland (15.9%) and Wales (22.3%) and lower rates in the Midlands (7.2%), South West (7.8%), South East (6.7%) and London (6.3%) (**17**). Such industrial recovery as took place in the late 1920s and late 1930s divided the country roughly into two parts contrasting depressed areas in the North and Wales with regions of comparative affluence in the Midlands, the South and the East.

The explanation of this division was evident to a traveller like J.B. Priestley. He saw the contrasting faces of old and new industrial areas [doc. 2]. The high unemployment in the North of England, in Scotland and in Wales reflected the concentration in these depressed areas of the staple industries of coal, cotton, iron and steel and shipbuilding. In the North East were coal mines, iron and steel works and shipbuilding firms [doc. 4]. In the North West were the cotton towns as well as considerable coalfields, some iron and steel companies and shipbuilding firms [doc. 3]. Shipbuilding, coal and iron and steel dominated southern Scotland, and South Wales relied on coal and iron and steel. These industries had developed in the nineteenth century and had attracted large populations, heavily dependent on them. When markets were lost at home and overseas, high structural as well as cyclical unemployment was unavoidable. By contrast in the Midlands and especially in the South and East other industries expanded, survived the cyclical depressions and created a new and more affluent Britain. In these favoured areas factories produced a range of modern consumer goods like electrical equipment and motor cars in newer cleaner buildings, using electrical power, not coal and steam, and drawing round them suburbs of new housing. Employment prospects here were brighter: nearly half the new factories opened in great Britain between 1932 and 1937 were in Greater London alone (53) [doc. 5].

It followed from the structural nature of their industrial problems that long-term unemployment, which created especially serious social problems, was largely concentrated in the depressed areas. In the summer of 1937 the long-term unemployed formed 25 per cent of the unemployed in the North West, 33 per cent in Scotland, 39 per cent in Wales and 40 per cent in the North. They made up only 8 per cent of the total in London, 10 per cent in the South East and 12 per cent in the South West (17).

Regional rates of unemployment disguised variations between towns in the same region. Workers were more liable to unemployment and especially to long-term unemployment if their town was heavily dependent on a single industry whose markets were severely reduced. A more diversified local economy with alternative occupations or a local industry whose products remained popular offered more favourable employment prospects. This could create prosperous towns even in depressed areas: in 1937 Halifax's machine tool trade kept unemployment down to 6 per cent and Consett's uniquely flourishing iron and steel industry in Co. Durham held local rates down to 5.4 per cent. But where circumstances were particularly unfavourable unemployment in a town could be well above regional norms. The tin and engineering industry declined in Redruth to leave unemployment at 29 per cent in 1937, high above the average for Cornwall (2, 17). In a generally depressed region some single industry towns were left virtually derelict. In August 1922 the shipbuilding town of Barrow-in-Furness had an unemployment rate of 49 per cent. Palmer's shipyard closed at Jarrow in the summer of 1934: 72.9 per cent of the workforce was unemployed in September 1935 [doc. 24]. In Blackburn where 60 per cent of jobs were in the cotton industry, the slump in 1931 left 46.8 per cent of workers unemployed. The South Wales coal mines had produced mainly for exports: lost markets created 61.9 per cent unemployment in Merthyr Tydfil in 1934 (2, 11, 30, 58). In such blackspots long-term unemployment was a natural corollary. It was extremely bad in some towns. In Crook, where the coal industry had collapsed, 71 per cent of the unemployed in November 1936 had been out of work for over five years. In Rhondda urban district they formed 45 per cent of the total (50).

Towns in which unemployment was high usually suffered from other consequences of economic depression. Workers still employed might not be employed for a full week: short-time working reduced their earnings. Wage rates were also lowered in industries hit by depression. Together with unemployment these factors substantially reduced the income of people living in the town. The effect on other local industries, shops and services may be imagined. Depression spread. Many small businesses catering for the local market could not survive. Moreover, a town in which consumers had low purchasing power hardly encouraged firms in the area to expand. It also discouraged new companies from moving in. Higher average incomes and more affluent customers naturally attracted businessmen into the South and East instead of the North and Wales (2, 53). Furthermore, severe economic depression created serious social problems and attempts by local authorities to raise revenue to deal with these problems increased local rates. In the late 1920s rates in Merthyr Tydfil were 27s6d in the pound. In spite of government attempts from 1929 to relieve industry of the burden, high rates may well have been another economic deterrent to new investment in depressed areas (11, 40).

Business managers and their families could also think of non-economic reasons for siting their companies and their homes in, for example, the new suburbs of Greater London rather than in the blighted valleys of South Wales. The areas of heavy industry had never been noted for their visual charm. Unadorned by the prospect of adequate profits they looked even less attractive to the investor. Their ageing faces were ravaged by the detritus of industrial depression. Observers commented on the physical remains of industrial collapse. 'Silent rusting shipyards are not an inspiring spectacle' (51). The failure of small businesses was recorded in the closed and boarded up shops conspicuous in town centres. Priestley estimated that one out of every two shops in Jarrow was closed. In Wigan Orwell saw 'no very obvious signs of poverty except the number of empty shops' (47). Hutt counted twenty-three closed shops in Tonypandy, a small mining town in the Rhondda. The signs of disrepair, of peeling paint and broken slates, were other symptoms of industrial decay. Uncongenial surroundings discouraged investment (38).

High unemployment and urban decay inevitably also encouraged some people to leave. Between 1921 and 1938 the distribution of the population around the regions of Great Britain changed considerably. The areas of rapid population growth were the regions of new industrial expansion: population in the South East increased by 18.1 per cent, in the Midlands by 11.6 per cent. The old industrial regions, fast growing in the nineteenth century, were checked. The West Riding grew by only 6 per cent, Lancashire and Cheshire by 3.5 per cent and Scotland by 2.1 per cent. The population of Northumberland and Durham actually fell by 1 per cent and South Wales lost 8.1 per cent of its inhabitants. Some people escaped from the depressed areas by leaving Britain and emigrating, mainly to Empire countries. But in the 1920s total net emigration from Britain was only about 130,000 a year and in the 1930s when depression affected most of the world many of them returned; more people entered Britain than left in the 1930s (12). The different rates of regional population growth are therefore mostly to be explained by the movement of people from one area of Britain to another. Some workers expressed their feelings about employment prospects and the quality of life in the industrial areas of the North West, North East, Scotland and South Wales by leaving for the Midlands, South East, South West and especially for London and the Home Counties. Some were to find work in the motor industry in Oxford or Luton; many joined the ranks of the unskilled in London; miners from the depressed areas helped develop the more profitable coalfields of Kent. Not only might the migrants better themselves but they may have eased the competition for jobs in their old homes.

Other effects of the movement were less satisfactory. Too many of the newcomers could not find jobs to suit their skills and were forced to seek unskilled work. Competition for unskilled jobs even in the more prosperous areas was always high; at times of cyclical depression any increase in the local labour force was unwelcome: migration merely spread unemployment into other areas. This surplus labour possibly depressed wage rates; it could increase pressure on local welfare services, intensify the demand for housing and exacerbate problems of overcrowding. Inevitably some local inhabitants resented the new immigrants; anti-Welsh feeling was common. Such hostility and difficulty in finding jobs, coupled to understandable homesickness, persuaded many escapees to return to the grim if familiar depressed areas. From 1928 the government had assisted the transfer of workers from depressed areas [doc. 25] but by June 1937 35 per cent of the juveniles and 27 per cent of the adults they helped had gone home. Nor were contemporaries entirely happy about the effect of such migration on depressed areas themselves. It was obviously most difficult for the married man with family ties and financial commitments to leave home and it was extremely difficult for the elderly to find jobs if they did leave. Most people who left were therefore young, unmarried men. Would this process denude towns in the depressed areas of the young and the enterprising, those who might have helped create renewed prosperity at home, whose skills would be needed if investment was to be encouraged? Would their absence tend to leave an ageing population drawing disproportionately on local welfare services? A vicious spiral of economic and cultural decay would follow. What must the quality of life be in the Rhondda after 28 per cent of its population, 47,000 people, were lost from the urban district between 1921 and 1935 **(49)**?

Undoubtedly migration took away something of the vitality from the worst hit places, but the remarkable feature of communities in the depressed areas seems to have been their resilience. It is surprising how many people chose to stay. The experience of unemployment was not so bad that people were forced out in desperation: welfare services provided some assistance, and the unemployed usually still had homes and personal possessions which they were reluctant to leave. But there was also a marked unwillingness to break out of the tight-knit cultural and social environment built up by the industrial working class in the nineteenth century and which now controlled and sustained them. Chapel, club and trade union did survive. Organisations to help the unemployed grew from local roots. If anything, especially in small towns, the more severe the depression the closer the community grew; unemployment was a shared experience and the financial and moral support of family, friends and local institutions persuaded many to stay. These were the ties which dissuaded most people from risking greater distress by leaving.

Who were the unemployed?

Losing and finding employment depended on other factors besides the area in which a man lived. A good deal was mere chance. Being on bad terms with a foreman was a disadvantage when work forces were being reduced. Being at the right gate at the right time or knowing someone who could pull strings or leak inside information was to be lucky when workers were being recruited. Since at best only one-third of the men who found work in the 1930s got their places through the official employment exchanges, such factors must have been important. It took Sam Grundy's influence at the city bus depot to rescue Harry Hardcastle and his father from unemployment **(17, 35)**.

Liability to unemployment also reflected personal characteristics. When the demand for labour fell it was inevitable that many of those who lost their jobs first and found new openings last suffered from disabilities. Their unemployment was personal, though it was cyclical depression or structural change which revealed how marginal was their membership of the labour market. The Pilgrim Trust investigators discovered a number of physically disabled long-term unemployed who suffered from industrial diseases or the consequences of accidents (50). It was also found in other studies that many long-term unemployed were physically out of condition or were at least assumed by employers to be unfit. Employers preferred to recruit new workers from those just out of work, believing that they would not have lost their health or skills (31). The less physically strong a man was the less likely he was to be re-employed, and the longer he remained unemployed the more his chances of being given a job dwindled. The long-term unemployed suffered additionally since personal appearance counted for a good deal when workers were selected. The longer a man was unemployed the more shabby his appearance became and frequently the more dispirited his manner. For similar reasons the mentally handicapped were barely members of the labour market in these years (50), and workers without any educational qualifications found themselves more vulnerable to unemployment (33).

Men were more prone to unemployment than women. There were of course far more male unemployed workers than female since the great majority of the work-force was male. But the rate of unemployment among male workers was also higher. In 1931 14.7 per cent of male workers were out of a job compared to 9.4 per cent of female workers. Since wage rates for women were substantially lower than those for men, employers sometimes preferred in a time of economic depression to jettison male employees rather than female ones if it was practicable. This often meant that a wife, a sister or a daughter might be employed when a husband, a brother or a father might be left unemployed at home. However, the problems faced by women were greater than this might suggest. Unemployment among *married* women was high: such workers were often the first to be dismissed in depression. Moreover women resembled, in one sense only, the physically and mentally handicapped: except in areas like Lancashire, where women traditionally worked in the textile industry, they tended to be only marginally members of the labour force. Social custom encouraged women to work only when single. When job opportunities shrank in the depression many women simply dropped out of the labour market and ceased to register at labour exchanges. Furthermore government legislation in

1931 deprived married women of entitlement to unemployment benefit and so they often ceased to register as unemployed. The figures for female unemployment therefore underestimate the real effects of the depression on women's employment (1, 7).

Age was another factor which crucially affected vulnerability: unemployment was at its lowest among juveniles but numbers rose rapidly between the ages of eighteen and twenty-four. The misfortune of many young men was to have embarked as juveniles on dead-end jobs: there were many unskilled jobs in which a boy could earn a fair wage but which led to dismissal at eighteen or twenty-one. In addition many boys seeking better careers signed up as apprentices between the wars, for example as engineers, to find not only that because of mechanisation they were no longer learning a particularly skilled trade but that when they finished their apprenticeship at the age of eighteen or twenty-one and could henceforth claim adult wages, their reward was dismissal. Cost-conscious employers preferred the cheap juvenile labour of apprentices of which there was a plentiful supply. Like Harry Hardcastle, the newly qualified engineer was very often an unemployed one (35). Employment prospects did not deteriorate much more between the ages of twenty-five and forty-four, but then came a new and more alarming danger. After the age of forty-five, the risk of a man losing his job did not increase the older he became, but the older he became, the less was his chance of finding another job should he become unemployed. Inevitably the amount of unemployment among older workers was higher: in 1931 when unemployment was around 13 per cent for men aged twenty-five to forty-four it was 22.6 per cent for men aged fifty-five to sixty-four. And of course the elderly man was most liable to long-term unemployment. They too had become marginal labour, disqualified by age from re-employment. Much of the bitterness and distress caused by unemployment was felt by men who knew themselves to be prematurely consigned to unrewarding and compulsory retirement. The only consolation was that many elderly workers tended not to have children still dependent on their support and that distress might have been much worse if younger men with families had been equally liable to high and long-term unemployment (1, 17, 50, 66).

Vulnerability also varied according to type of employment. As we have seen, the workers most affected were those in the old staple industries: miners, cotton operatives, shipbuilders and iron and steel workers. There were also large numbers of dock labourers and building workers. In the boom year 1937 these groups had unemployment rates of from 10 to 27 per cent, all above the national average. Unemployment was less a danger for workers employed on trams, buses and the railways, for those providing gas, water, electricity and distributive services, for printers and engineers and chemical workers, and for those making a range of consumer goods; here rates were below the national average. The long-term unemployed were distributed in similar fashion: in 1936 coalminers, shipbuilders, cotton workers, seamen and iron and steel workers headed the list with much lower rates recorded for other trades, including, it should be noted, dock labourers and building workers whose high unemployment rate was created by casual and seasonal factors and not by the structural problems mainly responsible for long-term unemployment (7, 50) [doc. 6].

One important feature of this pattern of unemployment was the critical situation for workers in the staple industries, many of whom in the nineteenth century had formed an aristocracy of skilled labour, for the most part well organised in trade unions, enjoying reasonable wages and security. Their fall was far and frightening, and this had important social consequences. However, an analysis of occupations affected by unemployment shows that unskilled workers were much more liable to become unemployed than those who were skilled. In 1931 30.5 per cent of unskilled manual workers in England and Wales were unemployed whereas only 14.4 per cent of skilled and semi-skilled manual workers were out of a job. Similarly an analysis of the long-term unemployed shows that unskilled workers had three times the unemployment rate of skilled and semi-skilled workers (31, 50). It is true that one effect of the depression had undoubtedly been the flooding of the unskilled labour market. Some former skilled workers finding no openings for their trade scrambled for jobs at lower levels and registered if necessary as merely general labourers; this artificially pushed up the totals of unemployed unskilled workers (31). Nevertheless in considering the further social effects of unemployment we need to remember that those out of work were predominantly unskilled. It is also evident that white-collar workers such as clerks and shop assistants were much more secure in their jobs, with rates of unemployment in 1931 of 5 to 8 per cent; managers, farmers and owners of shops and businesses were hardly affected with figures of ½ to 2 per cent (7).

Poverty

Contemporaries were anxious to discover not merely which workers were liable to unemployment and why, but wanted to trace the effects of unemployment on them. To what extent did the loss of a job plunge working-class families into poverty? Building on prewar studies, investigators in the 1920s and 1930s calculated a poverty line as the minimum income needed to meet essential family expenditure after the payment of rent. This involved calculating the cost of heating, lighting, clothing, household equipment, some additional running costs and the food required to meet basic nutritional needs. Families not having this minimum income were classed as living in poverty. Conclusions naturally varied according to estimates of essential needs, the area studied and the year of the survey. But all surveys agreed that in spite of improvements since before the war poverty was widespread even by the most exacting of standards. The most complete study was that carried out by Rowntree in York in 1936. He found that 31.1 per cent of working-class families lived in poverty. Applying Rowntree's standards to the evidence produced by other surveys of Merseyside, Southampton, London and Bristol in the late 1920s and the 1930s, we find between 15 and 30 per cent of working-class families in these towns without an income to meet minimum needs. It should be noted that none of these interwar surveys examined the extent of poverty in the most seriously depressed areas, and it is likely that conditions there were worse (15, 52, 57).

How far was unemployment responsible for the poverty discovered? Prewar studies had identified low wages as by far the most important single cause of distress and unemployment had not been a pre-eminent problem. The interwar surveys agreed that although low wages still caused much poverty, unemployment had become very serious. Rowntree concluded that 32.8 per cent of the poverty of York in 1936 was due to low wages and that 28.6 per cent was caused by unemployment; in London in 1928, casual work and low wages caused about 14 per cent of the poverty in the city but about 35 per cent was due to unemployment; in prosperous Bristol in 1937 21.3 per cent of poor families suffered because of low wages and 32.1 per cent because of unemployment (15, 52, 57). There is also some evidence to show that especially in the badly stricken areas, high unemployment levels depressed wage rates or encouraged short-time working to spread the work available. This reduced earnings. Unemployment may be regarded as one cause of low wages and therefore indirectly as well as directly a cause of poverty (2).

The same grim link between unemployment and poverty was revealed by examining the standard of living of unemployed families. Rowntree found that 72.6 per cent of unemployed workers lived below his poverty line. Even by the more spartan standards adopted in the Pilgrim Trust report, 30 per cent of families hit by long-term unemployment were below the poverty line and a further 14 per cent existed on it, and another study of Sheffield in the winter of 1931–2 found 42.8 per cent of the families of unemployed workers lived in poverty. It should be emphasised that these calculations assumed the most rigorous housekeeping, the most careful expenditure of income by the unemployed, no waste, no entertainments, no travel: a standard of existence not a standard of living. The numbers breaking the rules and suffering the consequences in poorer diet or shabbier clothing must have been considerable (48, 50, 52).

For most workers unemployment brought a serious fall in family income. A survey of about 800 families in Stockton-on-Tees in the early 1930s revealed that the average income of families where the wage earner was unemployed was 29s 2½d (£1.46) a week; where there was no unemployment it was 51s 6d (£2.57½). The Pilgrim Trust investigators calculated the average unemployment assistance allowances given by the government to the long-term unemployed and compared them with the previous average earnings of these workers. They found that allowances were between 45 and 66 per cent of previous wages, varying according to age. The drop in income was confirmed in a Ministry of Labour study in 1937 which showed that the average weekly unemployment insurance benefits paid to adult men was 24s 6d (£1.22½), whereas the median wage rates of these men when last employed was 55s 6d (£2.77½) (41, 50, 56).

Observers noticed that the longer unemployment lasted the sooner savings were used up and the more the consequences of a drop in income were exposed. Severe household economies followed: less use was made of coal, gas or electricity for cooking, heating or light; furniture was sometimes sold, pots and pans wore out and were not replaced; clothing suffered next – the shabbiness of unemployed families was conspicuous, and secondhand clothes had to be acquired [doc. 7]. Families ran into debt and piled up arrears of rent. Some were evicted; others moved into houses with lower rents, often sharing with other families. Lower incomes involved changes in diet: meat, milk and fresh vegetables were cut down or out; more potatoes, bread and margarine were eaten, stodgy foods which poorer families traditionally ate to stave off the feeling of hunger (30, 31, 46, 50). These were the most striking signs of falling living standards, but to them can be added the sight of unemployed workers trying to supplement their meagre incomes. They might be seen begging for the most casual of jobs, carrying bags at railway stations for example. For many people in the South East the most direct evidence of the distress of the depressed areas was the appearance of unemployed Welsh miners singing for coppers in London streets [doc. 8].

Some contemporary commentators concluded that national welfare services were inadequate since they did not prevent unemployed people from dropping below the poverty line. Charities distributing clothing and food could not deal with mass unemployment. Local authorities provided more valuable help: in some towns poor children were given free meals through the schools, and the poor law administered in the 1920s by Boards of Guardians and in the 1930s by Public Assistance Committees gave some financial help to unemployed families. But these measures varied from area to area and were not designed to cope with persistent depression. The principal cause of the poverty of so many unemployed families seemed to lie in the inadequacy of the state-run unemployment insurance scheme.

The original Act of 1911 was greatly extended in the early 1920s to cover most manual workers, to extend the period of benefit and to provide allowances for dependent wives and children. The major criticism made of the scheme was that the level of benefits was too low. Benefits paid between the wars were higher than before 1914 and their real value rose in the 1920s and early 1930s when prices fell, but the state made no attempt to guarantee that the level of benefits was sufficient to keep the unemployed and their families out of poverty (67).

Some commentators believed that benefits were just about adequate, but others like Rowntree and Tout were more critical. Unless the unemployed man had savings or other sources of family income Rowntree believed he was likely to fall into poverty. In 1936 an unemployed single man would receive 17s (85p) unemployment insurance money or a maximum of 15s (75p) unemployment assistance benefit if he had exhausted his normal insurance entitlement. Out of this he had to pay for his food, heating, household equipment, personal sundries and rent. Rowntree estimated that such an unemployed man needed 22s 9d (£1.13½) *plus* money for rent if he was to meet his minimum needs. A married couple, both unemployed, received 26s (£1.30) insurance benefit, or a maximum of 24s (£1.20) unemployment assistance relief and needed, according to Rowntree, 27s 8d (£1.38½) plus money for rent. A man, wife and three children would receive 35s (£1.75) insurance money, probably 37s 6d (£1.87½) from the Unemployment Assistance Board, and needed 40s 5d (£2.02) plus money for rent, perhaps 53s (£2.65) in all (52). It seemed obvious to Tout that many families of the unemployed were in poverty 'because benefit and relief scales are below the survey scale of "needs"' (57).

The Pilgrim Trust investigators had a lower standard for poverty and suggested that a married couple drawing unemployment assistance could keep on or above the poverty line, but they emphasised that with children such a family was likely to be in poverty. Mainly as a result they reckoned that 41 per cent of families wholly dependent on unemployment assistance for their income were living in poverty **(50)**. The more dependent workers were on such relief for their income, the more likely they were to be in poverty. When the level of benefits was cut in 1931 the damaging effect on living standards could be traced **(37, 55)**. In general many commentators agreed that state-provided unemployment relief was often inadequate to meet minimum needs, and unemployment did therefore force many families into poverty.

Distress was felt more severely by workers whose trades had in the past given them comparatively high living standards: skilled men like textile workers, steel workers, coalminers and shipbuilders experienced a particularly acute and painful drop in income. Many unskilled or semi-skilled workers had also been used to relatively good wages because of reasonable rates of pay and/or long hours. For such workers unemployment for all but the shortest periods brought a harrowing experience, life near or below the poverty line.

We must remember, however, that the majority of unemployed workers were unskilled and that many unskilled jobs were poorly paid. Low pay had been in the past the principal cause of poverty. Unemployment may well have affected such low-paid unskilled workers in a different way. According to the professed principles lying behind the unemployment insurance scheme, unemployment should have reduced the living standards of all workers. The nineteenth century doctrine of 'less eligibility' was supposed to guide interwar welfare provision. No worker ought to enjoy a higher income while unemployed than he had previously enjoyed while working. Otherwise the incentive to find work would be removed and disastrous social consequences were expected to follow. But in practice the levels of benefit paid under the Unemployment Insurance Acts were for some workers more attractive than the wages they had previously drawn or might expect to draw.

Some unskilled workers were used to casual, infrequent and low-paid employment; not only was their income low but it was irregular. However, if they qualified for insurance benefits or, from 1934, for unemployment assistance their standard of living could actually rise; their income would now be regular, allowing for more economy in their expenditure, and though allowances were low they might well be above their previous earnings. From its investigations of long-term unemployment, the Pilgrim Trust concluded that as many as 20 per cent of families dependent on unemployment assistance were as well off, or better off, than they would have been if at work **(50)**. The wages of

29

young people were notoriously low and this explains why one study in 1938 suggested that 20 per cent of unmarried youths received unemployment allowances at least as high as their last weekly wage; the same survey showed that because of dependants' allowances 50 per cent of married young men were at least as well off unemployed as employed (33). While wages were paid on a flat rate basis, unemployment relief was adjusted to take some account of family needs. For low-paid workers of all ages the extra dependants' allowances could make unemployment financially more attractive than work. The case was even stronger for low-paid workers with children. The Pilgrim Trust investigators described how an unskilled man might earn as little as 25s (£1.25) a week and not more than 40s (£2) a week, whereas if he had a wife and family he might draw 45s (£2.25) a week or more. As an extreme illustration they described the case of one young man who had not worked since he left school but who had found the energy to be married and the father of three children by the age of twenty. If he worked he might earn at most about 20s (£1) a week; unemployed, he drew 35s (£1.75) (50).

Such cases modify the impression derived from interwar reports that the poverty of unemployed families was always *caused* by their loss of a job. For the majority of workers this was undoubtedly the case, but for a substantial minority of the unemployed, poverty was the normal condition of their existence. Low wages and the burden of large families would in any case have subjected them to distress. Moreover, if some of the unemployed were better off living on unemployment relief, it shows that the state welfare system, though inadequate, did act as a low but effective safety net: it prevented unemployed workers from falling into the dire want which had been so common among the low paid before 1914. In spite of the poverty to which the depression condemned so many working-class families between the wars, they found themselves because of unemployment insurance with a standard of living at least a little better than that of most *employed* unskilled labourers before the war (4).

Health

Contemporary investigations into the living standards of the unemployed frequently raised another question. Did the health of unemployed workers and their families deteriorate? This consequence might seem unavoidable. During the interwar years more sophisticated knowledge was acquired of the connection between diet and health. In 1933 the British Medical Association published an analysis of the minimum diet which provided the calories, proteins and vitamins essential to maintain health. Social investigators like Rowntree worked out the cost of this or similar diets and incorporated results in their calculations of the minimum income which defined the poverty line. Since many, though not all, families were forced below the poverty line through unemployment it seemed likely that they would have to economise on food; their diets would be inadequate and their health must be in jeopardy.

Analysis of the food actually eaten by the families of unemployed workers seemed to confirm this. It frequently showed a high consumption of bread, margarine, potatoes, sugar and tea and an inadequate consumption of meat, vegetables, fruit and milk [doc. 9]. A study in Lincoln in 1936 concluded that 17 per cent more bread was eaten by the families of those out of work than by those employed, but that the unemployed man consumed only 38 per cent of the amount of milk consumed by the employed worker and 77 per cent of the amount of meat. The calorie and protein content of meals was therefore often below the amount consumed by employed families and less than the required amounts set down by nutritional experts. Many investigators noticed that the diets of wives and mothers were most seriously inadequate, priority being given to the meals of children and husbands (32, 42, 46, 50).

Yet many studies concluded that the evidence did not show any significant deterioration in the health of the unemployed. An enquiry into the effects of unemployment undertaken in the autumn of 1922 concluded that as a result of insurance benefits, poor relief and free schools meals, 'health has been maintained unimpaired' (30). A study made in Greenwich in 1931–2 agreed that there was no widespread deterioration in health through malnutrition, and added that 'so far as physical condition was concerned, it would be impossible on first observation to distinguish the average unemployed person from the person at work'. An unemployed engineer told the reporter: 'Unemployment benefit is not enough so's you can live like you're used to living. . . . But we get enough to keep us healthy, and you can't ask for much more, now, can you?' (31). This conclusion was supported by a Save the Children Fund enquiry which reported in 1931 on the health of the children in the families of the unemployed: 'It can be definitely stated that there has been no general deterioration' (55); nor could a study of Sheffield's unemployed trace any marked decline in health (48).

Such testimony must have been gratifying to interwar governments. They were reluctant to initiate investigations into the condition of the unemployed, and were provoked into making inquiries mainly by pessimistic and angry critics. A Labour Party pamphlet of 1928 entitled *The Distress in South Wales: health of mothers and babies imperilled* was answered by a Ministry of Health examination of conditions in the area. There was evidence, it agreed, of inadequate diet, but it concluded that at least at present there was no indication of a widespread deterioration in health (42) [doc. 10]. The Chief Medical Officer of the Ministry of Health took the same generally optimistic view in his annual report in 1934. Mortality rates were not held to be significantly higher in the depressed areas than elsewhere in the country and though infant mortality was much higher there than the national average this was not a new development attributable to the depression (34). A vigorous condemnation of this complacency in *The Times* in December 1934, by an experienced doctor in Co. Durham, was countered by another Ministry of Health investigation of conditions in the county. It admitted that there was considerable subnormal nutrition but not a high incidence of 'true malnutrition'. It was claimed that analyses of the general mortality rate, the infant mortality rate and the death rate from bronchitis, pneumonia, scarlet fever, diphtheria and measles in the area proved there was no sign of a deterioration in health. Unemployment had for the most part done no more than slow down the conquest of tuberculosis; the rare occurrences of rickets discovered were caused by poor parental care and not by economic circumstances. Finally, since 75 per cent of the population were in good health, the impact of unemployment did not appear to be serious (43). The Minister of Health relied on such judgements when he claimed in 1933 that 'there is at present no available medical evidence of any general increase in physical impairment, sickness or mortality as a result of the economic depression or unemployment' (37).

These official statements were regarded as grossly complacent by other investigators. It was argued, for example, that there was a grim correlation between the depressed areas with high unemployment and regions of higher than average mortality rates. The infant mortality rate in the Home Counties in 1935 was 42 per 1000 live births but in Glamorgan it was 63 and in Durham and Northumberland 76, it was wiser to be born in Coulsdon and Purley which had an infant mortality rate of 32 rather than in Jarrow which had a rate of 114. Maternal mortality in 1936 was 0.89 per 1,000 births in Middlesex but 5.34 in Glamorgan and 5.60 in Durham. Deaths from diphtheria, tuberculosis, heart disease, bronchitis and pneumonia were all significantly higher in the North and in Wales (34, 56).

Local medical officers frequently reported on the poor health record of districts in the depressed areas, and some critics like Hannington and Hutt cited these reports as evidence of the damaging effects of unemployment (37, 38). This evidence is suggestive of the possible effects of unemployment on health but all it really *proves* is the extent of bad health in the depressed areas and it does not show that unemployment made people more susceptible to illness than they would have been if employed in those regions. The regional pattern of the nation's health was not necessarily a consequence of the regional distribution of high unemployment. Poorer health in the North and in Wales than in the country as a whole was a feature of the prosperous years of the nineteenth century as well as of the period of interwar depression. It could be explained as the consequence of a wide range of social, industrial and environmental factors such as the greater number of slum houses, more overcrowding, air pollution and low wages. High unemployment was probably an additional handicap but its effects cannot be deduced simply from regional mortality rates. The regional health pattern would not, and after the Second World War did not, even itself out completely if unemployment disappeared.

For some investigators the physical condition of the unemployed was convincing evidence of the evil effects of the depression on health. George Orwell was dismayed by the mere appearance of workers in the depressed areas. 'The results of all this', he wrote, 'are visible in a physical degeneracy which you can study directly, by using your eyes. . . . The physical average in the industrial towns is terribly low, lower even than in London. In Sheffield you have the feeling of walking among troglodytes.' He was particularly struck by the badness of people's teeth, a sign to him of the under-nourishment unemployment was causing (46). More scientifically the Pilgrim Trust investigators examined the health of the long-term unemployed in 1936 and calculated that only 58 per cent were fit, while 24 per cent were out of condition and 18 per cent were unfit or had obvious physical defects (50). The Ministry of Labour provided some disturbing evidence: in 1934, medical examination of a sample of short-term unemployed (men drawing insurance benefits) showed that 75.5 per cent were in good physical condition, but that only 59.9 per cent of the long-term unemployed (men drawing transitional benefits) were fit. This suggested that prolonged unemployment caused a deterioration in health (56). Another study in Stockton-on-Tees carried out by the local medical officer seemed to confirm this. Families of the unemployed were compared with those of employed workers: similar in most other respects, there was nevertheless between

1931 and 1934 a standardised death rate of 21.01 per 1,000 for the families of the employed and a grim 29.29 per 1,000 for the unemployed **(41)**.

It is difficult to shake off the feeling that this evidence points to unemployment as a cause of deteriorating health, but there remains an element of uncertainty. The poor physical condition and higher death rates, particularly of the long-term unemployed, leave undetermined which was cause and which was effect. Did long-term unemployment undermine health and increase death rates? Or were people with poorer health less likely to be re-employed and therefore more prone to long-term unemployment? We know that employers tended to choose new labour from the recently unemployed and from those who looked most fit. The poorer health record of the long-term unemployed may have been caused as much by this process of selection as by the damaging effects of poverty and malnutrition to which many of the unemployed were undoubtedly also prone.

What was needed was clear evidence to show whether or not unemployment caused a deterioration in the health of the unemployed and their families. There was a strong measure of agreement about the serious effects of mental strain on workers and their families. The failure to find work, the enforced idleness, the fall in living standards and the death of hope caused psychological stresses; in some cases these were so severe as to produce neurotic illnesses. The Chief Medical Officer of the Ministry of Health admitted in 1932 that prolonged unemployment was causing mental depression bordering on neurasthenia among some of the older men. An increase in neurotic maladies was observed by the Ministry's investigators in Co. Durham **(32, 43)**. This was an effect noted by other independent observers also. An early report in 1922 concluded that 'there is abundant evidence of worry and mental strain, which is in cases affecting health' **(30)** [**doc. 11**]; it was even suggested that 'the hopeless struggle combined with a sense of worthlessness and guilt may drive some to suicide' **(32)**.

The evidence also shows that the health of women did sometimes deteriorate in the depressed areas. As mentioned, there was a tendency for mothers in the families of the unemployed to feed their children and husbands first and to deny themselves adequate meals [**doc. 12**]. Even the Ministry of Health acknowledged that many women in the depressed areas suffered from languor and anaemia. There may have been other consequences. The special needs of pregnant women for milk, cheese, butter, eggs, liver, fish, fresh fruit and vegetables were often too expensive for many employed workers, and they were far beyond the reach of the wives of the unemployed. The Ministry of Health admitted in 1937 that in South Wales there had been an increase in maternal mortality rates in the industrial areas since 1928, but it denied that there was any correlation with economic depression (**44**). Its statistical juggling is not altogether convincing, and other investigators were certain that there was a strong link; the Pilgrim Trust, for example, saw a rise in maternal mortality as the most serious effect of unemployment on public health (**50**).

The effects of unemployment on children are less clear. There may have been some increase in infant mortality rates but the case is not overwhelming (**30, 37, 55, 56**). More certain is an increase in the liability of children to deficiency diseases caused by poor nutrition. The Ministry of Health admitted that malnutrition in the depressed areas caused some increase in rickets (**42**); the School Medical Officer for Cumberland reported in 1933 that 'there is evidence of a very definite increase, almost a dramatic increase, in the incidence of rickets amongst children of school age' (**37**). Some observers blamed the 10 per cent cut in unemployment benefits and the introduction of the family means test in 1931 for a deterioration in the health of children. The Save the Children Fund team reported more malnutrition in 1932 than in 1931 and concluded that 'it is difficult not to associate this deterioration with the reduction in the scale of Unemployment Benefits' (**55**). The Medical Officer for Preston wrote:

> Possibly at no period during the last five years has work at the Infant Welfare Centre been so difficult as during the latter part of 1932. . . . One cannot help thinking that the means test was the responsible factor. . . . No one can deny that the ex-baby and the toddler were both definitely much less robust, much more in need of medical attention, and much more prone to rickets than was the case two years ago (**37**).

Most commentators also agreed that inadequate diet and the idleness imposed on the normally active manual worker caused many of the unemployed to complain of feeling unwell and of being out of condition (**32, 40, 55**) [doc. 10]. There was evidence of anaemia among unemployed men in Co. Durham (**43**). It is significant that the unemployed attending Government Instructional Centres in the 1930s could at first perform only light work, and that men gained on average 7 lbs (3.17 kg) in weight during their three-months stay (**50**). Poor diets did make men less fit and did induce languor, but it seems likely that this most widespread effect of unemployment on health was not permanent; a return to work raised living standards for most workers and their health recovered.

The effects of unemployment on health were undoubtedly serious. Even the common minor ailments were distressing to the victims and there is some evidence of more disease and a higher death rate, at least in the worst years and in the most badly affected areas. But it should also be recognised that unemployment did not strikingly swell the mortality and morbidity rates of the nation or even of the depressed areas; death and disease did not savagely scythe through the ranks of the unemployed and their families.

Such damage as did occur exposed the weaknesses in existing welfare services. It was clear that unemployment insurance was not adequate to guarantee the preservation of health. Moreover welfare services provided by local authorities were often least satisfactory where most needed. Free school meals and milk for necessitous children were largely financed from local rates, and the depressed areas were the regions with the highest need for these facilities and the least resources to pay for them; a penny (½p) rate in Jarrow in the 1930s provided local authorities with between £350 and £450; in Holborn in London it generated £6,800. In Jarrow and in some other badly hit towns during the worst years local authorities were forced to make economies in school meals and milk services (55, 56, 58). Inadequate provision jeopardised health, and in the depressed areas improvements in health were certainly checked by the impact of unemployment. Nevertheless it is also clear that the services provided by central and local authroities prevented any dramatic deterioration in health standards: unemployment benefit, poor relief, free school meals and free milk plus general improvements in environmental and hospital health services between the wars prevented the sort of social disaster which chronic depression on the interwar scale would have caused in earlier decades.

Morale

Many of those who investigated the condition of the unemployed examined what they called the effects of depression on morale. This covered a range of topics. Most were concerned by the mental distress caused by unemployment. But many also wondered whether the experience of long-term and widespread unemployment was permanently destroying the hard-working, socially conformist, law-abiding and politically quiescent standards of traditional working-class behaviour.

All commentators agreed that a common consequence of unemployment was mental suffering. The Ministry of Health investigators in South Wales 'from the first . . . were struck more by the aspect of depression among the unemployed men and their listlessness than by any other sign of poverty' **(42)**. While the first week or so of unemployment could be treated as a holiday, it was abundantly clear that over a longer period the unemployed came up against the distinction between leisure and idleness. Only a few found unemployment a welcome release from work. Walter Greenwood records that 'to me the leisure which unemployment provided was anything but disagreeable. It brought a bubbling sense of freedom' **(98)**. Those with interests and mental equipment like Greenwood could find constructive and fulfilling use for their leisure in reading, writing, educational courses and in political activity. Others found satisfaction in the activities of unemployed men's clubs or the cultivation of allotments **(22, 23)**. But most found idleness a burden, the day a void to be filled.

There were a few activities common to most. There was the routine of queueing at the labour exchange, signing the register, drawing unemployment pay. The occasion had a social as well as financial value, bringing the unemployed together, providing an opportunity for talk, breaking down the isolation of the man without work. In the early weeks of unemployment the tramp from factory to factory in search of work absorbed much time and energy. As hope fell, expectations dropped and the search for work might degenerate into a desultory search for casual jobs.

One principal preoccupation was keeping warm. At home this could be expensive on fuel; hence the attraction of the public library, the clubs for unemployed men and the public lectures arranged by various societies and churches. In Sheffield Orwell sat through a clergyman's talk on 'Clean and dirty water': 'B. says that most of the members of this brotherhood are unemployed men who will put up with almost anything in order to have a warm place where they can sit for a few hours' **(47)**. Such ordeals provided some entertainment. The search for anodyne escapes like this was another major problem for the idle unemployed. Those who calculated poverty lines made no allowance for the unemployed man's need for distractions. While the morality of using dole money for betting was debated **(30)**, the desire for the excitement and stimulus of gambling received less attention. Only a few like Orwell saw that 'even people on the verge of starvation can buy a few days' hope ("Something to live for", as they call it) by having a penny on a sweepstake' **(46)**. The warmth and entertainment provided so cheaply by the cinema explain why as many as 80 per cent of unemployed youths in Liverpool and Glasgow went to the cinema at least once a week **(33)** [**doc. 13**]. But such distractions could not do more than relieve temporarily what Orwell noted as the 'deadening, debilitating effect of unemployment'. Boredom was the enemy, life became existence.

The distress caused by idleness underlined the importance of work to the working class. Work had three principal values. Most working people completely accepted the concept of work as a duty; skilled workers especially were proud of their work: employment gave a man status and respectability. Moreover work satisfied the social instincts of human beings: a man at work was a man with friends, a member of a social group, part of society. And, of course, work was rewarded with money. Without a job many workers, especially in the early years of the depression, felt acutely ashamed and humiliated. That they were out of work seemed a reflection on their character. They felt they lost status. Unemployment benefits seemed like poor relief or charity handouts, and dependence on them sapped self-respect (30, 33). Losing a job also severed the social connections developed at work, and with little in the pocket to pay for drinks in the pub it was difficult to maintain old associations out of working hours. At worst this led to the isolation of the unemployed worker. More commonly a single working-class society divided into two communities – the employed and the unemployed; their occupations and life styles differed and kept them apart. Observers noticed how friends could separate, how youths might drop their girlfriends, how the unemployed gathered together as a distinct social group, centred sometimes in their clubs, or on street corners, or in the dole queue (32, 33). The exultant Harry Hardcastle, re-employed and with his first pay packet, stole away guiltily down a back entry rather than face his still unemployed friend (35).

The tendency was most marked in the areas of reasonable prosperity. In those regions, the long-unemployed man was a more isolated figure, his 'failure' more apparent to him and to others, his poverty more conspicuous when set against the affluence of neighbours, his bitterness the greater. In the depressed areas, particularly in a small close-knit community, a South Wales mining town or a place like Jarrow, the depression was much more obviously a catastrophe for the whole community, unemployment more obviously no fault of the unemployed, and the experience common in many homes. Distress was great but adjusting to life on the dole was easier (50).

The signs that there was less mental distress in the most depressed towns was actually a source of worry to some observers. Was there less distress because the work ethic, the will to work, had been permanently eroded? Would there not be frightening social consequences if the unemployed were cheerfully adopting the life of a leisured class? As the depression dragged on through the 1930s the unemployed increasingly accepted public assistance without demur. 'Those who feel that there is an element of disgrace in receiving Unemployment Assistance are unusual', wrote the Pilgrim Trust reporters. A Rhondda miner told them: 'I can remember the days when it was thought shame to accept poor relief. Now there's so many do it that there is nothing to it' **(50)**. Orwell saw 'whole populations settling down, as it were, to a lifetime on the P.A.C.'. But he was one of the few who found it 'admirable, perhaps even hopeful, ... that they have managed to do it without going spiritually to pieces' **(46)**. The Pilgrim Trust report argued that 'for three and a half centuries one of the assumptions underlying Western individualism has been that a man was responsible for the maintenance of himself and his family'. They feared that the public relief of the unemployed might undermine this attitude **(50)**.

Some investigators were especially anxious about the younger generation. Young men, they argued, did not have years of work experience behind them and missed work less. They lacked the work ethic of their elders. Many of them were 'work-shy'; they seemed to adapt more easily to unemployment. They were a shaky foundation for the nation's future. It was for them that occupation centres and training schemes were most needed, to keep them physically and mentally fit for work — when work came. These conclusions were reached in a large number of contemporary reports **(30, 31, 33, 51, 55)**.

There is, however, plenty of evidence to show that only a few workers were content to accept relief rather than to seek work. Those who did were mainly unskilled workers whose work had in the past given them little satisfaction and low status and whose present unemployment money was about as much as their previous low pay. In general welfare services had not destroyed the will to work. 'Many workers, probably the great majority, prefer to work even if the financial gain from it is slight', admitted the Pilgrim Trust report **(50)**. Bakke wrote: 'The number of semi-skilled men with large families who said they would "jump at the chance" to go back to work, even if they received no more than their insurance benefit, is an indication that even in a machine age there are other rewards for work than the money reward.' One worker said: 'I don't care what your job is, you feel a lot more important when you come home at night than if you had been tramping around the streets all day' **(31)**. When work was available the unemployed were willing to take it, and there is no convincing evidence that high unemployment between the wars had any permanent effect on working-class attitudes to work.

There was a fear that the strains created by unemployment were causing widespread damage to family life. By tradition in most working-class families the husband/father was the master, the head of the household, but his status rested a good deal on his position as the breadwinner. The risk of long-term unemployment increased with age so that it was very often husbands and fathers who were out of work. Only in areas like South Lancashire where female employment was common (in the textile industry) was it more tolerable to let a woman be the principal wage-earner. But generally the loss of status and self-respect inevitably following from unemployment was more galling if wives or daughters remained in work; it was bitter enough for a man to be supported by the earnings of his son. Such dependence was exposed most woundingly when after 1931 unemployment allowances were related to household earnings. Once a worker had exhausted his rightful claim to insurance benefit, his dole money was reduced or cut altogether if the authorities reckoned that the earnings of other members of the family were sufficient to meet family needs. The enforced dependence on wife and children for support caused as much distress as the financial loss. One South Wales miner described himself as 'a pauper through having to depend upon my children for a living' (32). Similarly unemployed sons, and some unemployed daughters, felt themselves a drain on family income and resented their lost independence. Occasionally the tension was sufficient to destroy families: marriages were broken [doc. 14]; there were cases of elderly parents being forced out of family homes because their pensions reduced their children's dole under the means test; and unemployed sons, seeking independence, sometimes moved into lodgings. It was also sometimes said that social norms were being undermined because unemployed men were reluctant to marry (32, 33, 37, 46, 50).

Undoubtedly tragedies occurred and families were parted; moreover we must imagine many more occasions when enforced idleness, poverty, loss of self-respect and the disruption of normal family roles created more than the normal amount of tension in the confined and often over-crowded working-class house. But it is particularly striking how resilient most homes were in the crisis, and how normal the life their members tried to lead. There was not a striking increase in divorce rates until the 1940s, and one foreign study suggests that marriages which did crumble under the strain of unemployment were already fragile (8, 39). Family solidarity remained a source of help for most unemployed people; sometimes children living with their parents only left home in the sense that they acquired accommodation addresses and drew their full unemployment allowances as heads of a separate establishment. The Pilgrim Trust reporters found only a handful of cases in which the means test had really driven sons out of the family home (50).

Orwell was astonished to see how little change there was in the man's role in the home in spite of his unemployment. He might be idle but housework remained woman's work. The women, as well as the men, 'feel that a man would lose his manhood if, merely because he was out of work, he developed into a "Mary Ann"'. The desire for normal family life among the young was also apparent: marriage might be postponed, but it was not prohibited. Orwell commended their willingness to get married on the dole: 'It annoys the old ladies of Brighton, but it is a proof of their essential good sense; they realise that losing your job does not mean that you cease to be a human being.' His conclusion seems sound: 'the family-system has not broken up' (40, 46, 48).

Was unemployment with its attendant consequences of bitterness, a fall into poverty and idleness responsible for the rise in crime revealed in the criminal statistics between the wars? Some contemporary criminologists, prison commissioners and social investigators believed there was a connection (54). The annual report of the prison commissioners for 1922 argued that 'it is probably right to say that unemployment is one of the chief contributory factors to the prison population of today' (25), and the *Daily Mail* headed a story in 1926 'The Deadly Dole: From Idleness to Crime' (15). The Pilgrim Trust reporters and others came upon particular cases of unemployed workers turning to crime (50) [doc. 15].

Impressions of social trends can be misleading and the interpretation of criminal statistics is fraught with difficulties. It seems plausible that a fall in living standards induced some people to turn to crime. In the 1930s national figures suggest that unemployment and crimes by men over the age of twenty-one rose and fell together, but an examination of behaviour in particular towns showed no exact correlation. For example there was much higher unemployment in Gateshead than in Norwich between 1934 and 1936 but far less crime, and there was no increase in crime in Sheffield in 1931 although unemployment nearly doubled; furthermore juvenile delinquency continued to rise in the 1930s in spite of improvements in employment prospects which suggested other influences were at work. In brief, unemployment was probably one incentive to crime, but other factors such as general living standards in the area, police activity or nonconformist traditions would encourage or restrain criminal behaviour (25). The proven effects of unemployment on crime were by any calculation not great: there was no conspicuous breakdown of law and order in the depressed areas where it might be expected. On balance it seems proper to agree with those commentators who were struck by the law-abiding behaviour of most victims of unemployment. To such observers unemployment insurance, poor relief and other welfare services had at least 'prevented any serious breaking down among the needy of a respect for law' (30, 31, 55).

Did unemployment have a similarly negligible effect on political behaviour? Some commentators, especially left-wing ones, feared that unemployed working-men in the 1930s might be deceived into supporting Oswald Mosley's British Union of Fascists as the stormtroopers who would break up the Labour movement. Conversely, others, including politicians in office, trembled at the thought of Bolshevik agitators stirring up trouble among the misguided unemployed. This fantasy inspired the plot for Sapper's novel *The Black Gang* (1922) and it lay behind regular police reports to the cabinet on political activities among the unemployed. However the Fascist party remained small, 40,000 at most, of whom only about 10,000 were active members; it was not noticeably more successful in the depressed areas, and drew few recruits from unemployed manual workers (28, 107). Membership of the Communist Party never rose above 11,000 until anti-fascism attracted new recruits in the late 1930s and even then it was less than 18,000 in 1939; moreover, its tone was set more by leisured middle-class intellectuals than by unemployed workers (28).

More successful was the National Unemployed Workers Movement formed in 1921 by Wal Hannington, an unemployed Communist engineer. It organised a large number of local demonstrations and six impressive national hunger marches against unemployment and rates of benefit. Many of these protests ended in violent clashes between the demonstrators and the police. Government, police and press usually took an alarmist view of its work, exaggerating its influence, its communist connections and its revolutionary implications (29). The authorities monitored its activities through a police spy established in its directing council (24). But the NUWM was hardly revolutionary in its behaviour. It had communist links but it achieved popular support only when it drew attention to inadequate rates of unemployment relief. It did not even campaign vigorously for work for the unemployed let alone social revolution. It organised big demonstrations most successfully against such tangible enemies as the means test in 1931 and the policies of the new Unemployment Assistance Board in 1935. Although it was more active, it did little that was different in kind from the hunger marches and demonstrations organised by local groups as in Jarrow or, rather belatedly, by the TUC and the Labour Party. Many unemployed workers did attend these demonstrations, but membership of the

NUWM remained small, 50,000 at a period of peak activity in 1931 and 1932 when the unemployed numbered over 2½ million. Hannington was grossly exaggerating the strength of the movement when he admitted that it never recruited as much as 10 per cent of the unemployed (22, 28, 36).

It is clear that extremist political action attracted only a handful of the unemployed; demonstrators asked for more liberal relief not for social revolution. Poverty and bitterness had little political effect: unemployment seemed to induce in most of its victims a political apathy akin to the physical languor from which so many suffered [doc. 16]; it did not seem possible to get them to believe that unemployment was anything but an act of God against which no action was worthwhile (27). A South Wales miner admitted 'it has definitely lessened my interest in politics, because it has led me to believe that politics is a game of bluff, and that these people do not care a brass farthing for the bottom dog; it is only power which they seek' (32). This indifference may also be ascribed to the effects of existing relief measures. The absence of unrest was 'to be attributed to the success of the relief measures in meeting essential needs for food' (30).

The plain fact appears to be that there has been brought into the worker's life, even when he is unemployed, a sufficient degree of security, so that talk of undermining the social order which gives him even that small degree of security is an interesting debating opportunity rather than a vital discussion of actual possibilities (31).

One day in Wigan, Orwell went to an NUWM social evening. He found the gathering made up mostly of middle-aged women, young girls and old men; even the singing was excruciating. 'God help us,' he wrote, 'there is no *turbulence* left in England' (47).

The social consequences of unemployment naturally varied a great deal according to the cause and length of unemployment, the year, the place, the sex, age and occupation of the worker, his or her personality and family circumstances. Generalisation is difficult, but one impression stands out. Working people seem to have been extraordinarily resilient, or stubborn, in the face of the depression. Communities did not break up: there was migration but no mass exodus from the depressed areas. Unemployment brought poverty into many homes and physical and mental suffering too often accompanied it. But established patterns of working-class life survived; attitudes to work, roles in the family, respect for law and order and political behaviour were not substantially altered. This reflected in part at least the value of existing central and local government welfare services which prevented mass starvation and a savage deterioration in health. This is in no way to deny that unemployment caused real suffering. Liability to unemployment exacerbated the normal insecurity of working-class life; being out of work did cause real pain, mental at least as much as physical. These were wasted years of blighted lives. That such social distress was tolerated for so many years reflects badly on the operations of the British economy and on the quality of government between the wars.

4   Unemployment Policies

In the past, private philanthropic organisations and local authorities
played major roles in trying to tackle severe social problems in Britain.
But already in the decade or so before the First World War the central
government had tentatively accepted a responsibility to provide some
help for the unemployed on a national basis. Their troubles were to be
eased by the work of Labour Exchanges established in 1909, by unemployment insurance cover for some workers after 1911, and by some
small-scale public works schemes financed by the Unemployed Work-
men's Act of 1905 or the Development Fund set up in 1909. But
unemployment was still thought of mainly as a short-term if recurrent
social problem, and its prevention or relief were not regarded as major
central government duties (60, 65).

Severe depression between the wars changed that. It is true that
private philanthropy again responded to social crisis. Indeed one
historian has suggested that 'in alleviating the suffering of those out of
work the state's efforts were overshadowed by those of a voluntary
nature' (23). Handouts of clothes and food, educational classes, allotments and free holidays were provided by organisations like the National
Council for Social Services and the Workers' Educational Association.
Most common were the voluntary occupation centres where many unemployed workers found a social life, recreational facilities and the
equipment for woodworking, cobbling, tailoring or other useful hobbies.
At their peak between 1936 and 1938, these centres claimed a membership of about 200,000 [doc. 17]. In addition some local authorities
strained their financial resources to provide relief works, to distribute
food and clothing and above all to give financial help under the poor
law (40, 48). But valuable though these activities were, they did not
eliminate the distress caused by unemployment and certainly could
not remove its economic causes. The longer the depression lasted the
more serious did its nature seem, and the more unsuitable did established
methods of dealing with the problem appear. The state was pressed
to extend its responsibilities. These years were a time of painful educa-
tion and experiment.

The Effects of Economic Depression

1920–1925

The period stretching from the onset of depression in 1920 to the return to the gold standard in 1925 may be regarded as a unit. There were rapid changes of government in these years but this had little effect on the character of government economic and welfare policies designed to deal with unemployment. The Coalition administration of Lloyd George (1918–22), the Conservative governments of Bonar Law (1922–3) and Baldwin (1923–4), Labour's first government under Ramsay MacDonald (1924), and Baldwin's second government (1924–9), especially in its early months, had generally similar aims and policies.

All administrations between 1920 and 1925 shared the same interpretation of the causes of high unemployment. According to orthodox economic theory as developed by nineteenth-century economists, there could be no such thing as a permanent economic depression. In a depression supply exceeded demand, but this, it was argued, could only be temporary, since theory comfortingly explained how on balance economic production generated enough purchasing power as wages, salaries and profits for demand always to equal supply. As a result all factors of production tended to be fully occupied: labour like capital would be fully employed; unemployment could therefore only be temporary, due mainly to frictional problems or more seriously to the trade cycle (**80**). The depression beginning in 1920 was, it was true, exceptionally severe, but understandably it was assumed that this was merely another temporary cyclical depression as experienced before the war. Its severity was explained by certain economic dislocations at home and overseas caused by the economic effort of the First World War and the political consequences of its settlement. Since all industrial nations were in difficulties in the immediate postwar years, it was not recognised that Britain had a special structural economic problem involving a permanent fall in demand for the products of her staple industries.

This common explanation of the depression was followed by a general agreement on the solution. Unemployment would disappear when an upturn in the trade cycle brought recovery to the export industries especially of coal, cotton, iron and steel and shipbuilding. Governments believed they could best help by trying to restore pre-1914 conditions. That meant reviving the free market economy at home, while seeking to restore the international financial and trading system abroad.

It may be thought surprising that the Labour government conformed to the pattern. After all, the Labour Party had in 1918 formally committed itself for the first time to an explicit socialist programme and claimed in the 1923 general election that only Labour had 'a positive remedy' for unemployment (84). The orthodoxy of the Labour government in 1924 was not a consequence of its minority status, dependent though it was on Liberal support for its majorities in the House of Commons. Its behaviour, like that of its successor of 1929–31, followed from the conception of socialism held by the leadership and much of the party. The trouble with capitalism lay in its distribution of profits, the inequality of shares between employers and employees. Capitalism was immoral. But there were few who claimed that capitalism as an economic system did not work and was doomed to failure. Labour believed that socialism would evolve out of successful liberal capitalism, with the state gradually ensuring a fairer distribution of wealth. The party leaders therefore had no special plans with which to construct socialism in years when capitalism was doing badly and generating such high unemployment. They were left with the ironic problem of having to restore capitalism before they could move on to socialism, and rather lamely followed the orthodox policies which the establishment claimed would lead to the recovery of the capitalist economy (71, 79) [doc. 18]. Hence the general uniformity in these years between the policies of all governments.

It is apparent that in the gloom of the 1920s, the years before the war acquired a roseate glow which blinded observers to the darker aspects of Britain's earlier economic performance: the structural problem from which the British economy was beginning to suffer even before 1914 was obscured. It is also clear that the government regarded private enterprise as the main agent of economic recovery and minimised its own role. This is the more surprising since the First World War had required a gigantic and not unsuccessful experiment in state economic management. Government expenditure had soared, taxation had risen, production, prices and labour were subjected to state control. But after November 1918 it was widely argued that the emergency had passed and with it the justification for state domination of the economy. State controls were rapidly demolished (11, 16).

The government's primary aim after 1918 was to remove those dislocations caused by the war which seemed to be hindering the 'normal' recovery of trade. At home, even before the depression struck, the main problem was thought to be high prices. When the war ended wholesale prices were 140 per cent above the level of July 1914 and unwise government action in 1919 allowed them to rise even higher (12). When unemployment began to rise the government became even more worried by inflation. High prices reduced demand at home and, more seriously, were thought to price British goods out of foreign markets. Without a reduction in prices how could British exports recover and unemployment be relieved?

In explaining this rise in prices much attention was focused on wages. During the war full employment and a rising cost of living had pushed up wage rates considerably. By 1920, following more increases during a year of economic boom, money wage rates were nearly three times the level of 1913. Orthodox economists and most employers argued that the high cost of labour was greatly responsible for high prices and therefore for lost markets, and that until wage levels came down, unemployment would stay up. Ministers publicly supported this argument and sat back, while in a series of strikes in the early 1920s trade unions fought unsuccessfully to resist wage reductions. By 1923 wage rates were on average down to nearly two-thirds of their 1920 level (2, 11).

Governments had more direct responsibility for another cause of high prices. Central government expenditure had been less than £200 million in 1913–14, but in each of the last two years of the war it was over £2,500 million. This expenditure was especially inflationary because over the years 1914–15 to 1919–20 nearly two-thirds of it had been met by government borrowing. The total debt piled up by these unbalanced budgets came to over £7,000 million. After the war Chancellors of the Exchequer were obsessed by the size of this debt and they devoted most of their time to trying to deal with it (68). They also condemned high taxes as a cause of high prices. Income tax had gone up from 1s 2d (6p) in the £ before the war to 6s (30p) in the £ by 1920–1, and this and other taxes were passed on by producers as higher prices. The trouble had been caused mainly by the substantial increase in the national debt brought about by government borrowing. Annual interest payments on this debt had been only £20 million in 1913 but by 1920 they totalled £325 million and absorbed nearly one-third of the yield from taxation. Chancellors were horrified (12, 68, 81).

The solution seemed straightforward. If prices were to be reduced and trade was to recover, government expenditure would have to be drastically cut back so that budgets would either balance or would preferably leave a surplus each year. Additional government debts could then be avoided, some of the national debt could be paid off and taxes could be reduced. An 'anti-waste' campaign in the press and in the House of Commons reinforced the advice of the Treasury and persuaded Lloyd George's government to follow this orthodox policy in its response to unemployment in 1921 [doc. 19]. Later administrations stuck to it. Between 1920 and 1925 government expenditure was cut by about a quarter in real terms, budgets generated surpluses, some of the national debt was paid off and taxes were reduced a little; income tax for example was down to 4s (20p) in the £ by 1925. Unfortunately it is now apparent that while a reduction in taxation was a help to an economy in depression, cuts in government expenditure, just like wage reductions, tended to reduce the level of domestic demand for industrial goods. Far from assisting recovery, at least in the early years of the depression, the government's deflationary policy was probably making unemployment worse (2, 68, 69).

The policy, however, had an extra appeal because it seemed to offer other advantages to industrial producers. It was always assumed by the orthodox between the wars that industrial capital was scarce. It was argued that the money people saved was always taken up as capital for investment and that one thing which was reducing the amount of capital on the market was the high taxation which limited savings. Another limitation on the amount of capital available to industry was the extent of government borrowing. If government borrowed money, then less would be left for private enterprise. It followed that taxes should be kept low and government borrowing should be avoided. As Baldwin told his cabinet colleagues in a memorandum he wrote as Chancellor in 1922: 'Money taken for Government purposes is money taken away from trade, and borrowing will thus tend to depress trade and increase unemployment' (104). This erroneous thesis was soon to be challenged, as we shall see, by critics of government policy.

The attack on high prices at home was also regarded as essential as preparation for the removal of what many thought to be the major obstacle to prosperity. During the war Britain and other countries had suspended the gold standard which had governed international exchanges up to 1914. After the war, wild inflation and unstable exchange rates made any return to it impossible. Britain herself formally left the gold standard in 1919 because prices at home were too high in comparison with American prices to maintain the prewar parity of $4.86 to the £. However, even at the moment of departure Lloyd George's government expressed its determination to return to the gold standard at the prewar parity when circumstances permitted. One essential requirement was a substantial reduction in prices in Britain relative to those in the United States. Later governments piously accepted the need for the gold standard and for the generally deflationary policy which would make it practicable. It was accepted as a necessary goal by the Labour Chancellor in 1924, and Churchill received widespread support when he announced the decision to return at the prewar parity in his budget speech in April 1925. To a considerable extent the restoration of the gold standard was the dominant objective of economic policy in the 1920s.

Many historians have argued that the decision to return to gold disregarded the needs of British industry and the problem of unemployment. 'It was', writes Professor Pollard, 'essentially a bankers' policy, not directly concerned with industry at all' (77). Strong pressures for a return, particularly at the prewar parity, undoubtedly came from the City of London: such a restoration of the old order would revive the prestige of sterling and, it was hoped, the position of London as the financial centre of the world. The profits of the City had before 1914 been of major importance, not just to the financiers who lived on them, but to the nation's balance of payments. It may be that this factor, explained to governments by the siren voices of financiers and especially of Montagu Norman, the Governor of the Bank of England, strongly influenced monetary policy. But ministers and their advisers frequently coupled the financial arguments with industrial ones: according to Professor Sayers, 'the gold standard policy was essentially an employment policy' (78).

In the 1920s it was widely believed that British exports had done so well before the war because nations were joined together by the international gold standard. This it was claimed made international payments straightforward and encouraged the multilateral trade links from which British industry benefited. The destruction of the international gold standard was thought to be greatly responsible for the dislocation of international trade, and therefore a major cause of the troubles of Britain's export industries and of high unemployment. The industrial advantages of a return to gold were strongly emphasised by Churchill's Treasury advisers (75) [doc. 20].

The industrial case for a return was unfortunately not very closely argued. It failed to see that the international gold standard before the war was largely founded on Britain's ability to lend large amounts of capital overseas, and was therefore more a consequence than a cause of Britain's uniquely successful export-based economy. Supporters of the gold standard asserted rather than proved that a return to gold, particularly at prewar parity, would help the ailing postwar export industries, and they failed to see that Britain lacked the resources to support the system. Moreover, the emphasis was placed on the value of restabilising links with markets overseas and too little attention was paid to the possibly damaging effects a return would have on the market at home. As already mentioned, the deflation necessary to reduce British prices hurt the domestic economy. Furthermore, although partly offset by open market operations, the high bank rate needed after 1925 to attract foreign funds and so defend the vulnerable £ probably discouraged industrial investment. It is also likely that at $4.86 the £ was overvalued, perhaps by 10 per cent. Set against the substantial structural problems of the British economy these inconveniences were certainly not the burdens which decisively weighed down the British economy as some commentators and later historians claimed, but they were extra handicaps British businesses could ill afford **(69, 75)**. More seriously, committed to this fixed exchange system, the government could not use monetary policy in a more flexible way to stimulate economic recovery, either by lowering the bank rate or by devaluation. But this was one attraction of the policy to decision-makers at the time; it allowed the government to shake off the burden of economic management by reviving what was supposed to be an automatic self-regulating international exchange system. In the 1920s ministers wished to avoid responsibilities, believing that international trade like domestic industry flourished best when left free. This was clear evidence of a desire to return to the prewar days of the liberal free market economy, years in which unemployment had not been a major headache.

A proper restoration would require a good deal of international cooperation. Much of British foreign policy in these years aimed at persuading other nations to join in the reconstruction of the international economic system. British ministers were anxious to revive traditional British markets in Europe, especially in Germany and in Russia, much disrupted by war and revolution. What was immediately required was a settlement of the vexed question of Allied reparations claims on Germany and some solution to the problem of international war debts. The revival of the international gold standard ought to be possible once national economies were more stable, and the achievement of good international relations should help this. Few of these difficulties had been entirely solved by 1925. The French occupation of the Ruhr in 1923 seriously set back German economic recovery and the cause of international peace. At the Genoa conference in 1922 nations pledged themselves only to the principle of restoring the gold standard. In 1923 Baldwin negotiated a settlement of Britain's war debt with the United States, but such debts continued to embitter international relations and complicate trade. A trade treaty with Russia in 1921 suggested a revival of normal relations across the great divide, but as the Labour government found to its cost in 1924, Anglo-Russian relations were fraught with complications. Yet something had been achieved. After hard work by MacDonald, the Dawes Plan was accepted in 1924 as a settlement of the reparations problem; by 1925 Germany's economy was reviving, and a new international harmony seemed to have been achieved by the Treaty of Locarno in that year **(16, 71, 104)**. Nevertheless, although there was the beginning of a considerable economic upswing overseas, especially in the United States, Britain seemed to obtain little benefit from it. Unemployment statistics stubbornly registered the failure of Britain's exports to recover.

International diplomacy was symptomatic of a government strategy which aimed primarily at the resurrection of an economic order in which private businesses could revive unhampered and unguided by government interference. It followed that ministers in these years gave very little direct help to industries; they were persuaded to give some assistance, especially to the export industries, but their aid was noticeably cheap. Immediately after the war the government tried to encourage British exporters by guaranteeing the credits they gave to foreign buyers and this system was extended by Acts in 1920 and 1921. With the same aim, under the Trade Facilities Acts of 1921, 1922 and 1924, government guarantees slightly cheapened the loans raised by approved companies. As an extra bonus the act of 1924 allowed the government to pay three-quarters of the interest on these loans for five years. Financially these measures cost very little and economically their effects were not significant **(2, 62)**.

The same reluctance to spend can be seen in the government's refusal to reduce unemployment by large-scale relief works. There were small prewar precedents for initiating public works as a way of relieving unemployment, but in spite of high postwar unemployment governments did little to extend the policy. When unemployment first became a public issue in the winter of 1920–1, the government set up the Unemployment Grants Committee but even by 1928 it had provided direct employment for only about 4 per cent of the unemployed. A little additional employment was deliberately created in the early 1920s when government departments, like the Ministry of Transport, accelerated their building programmes **(30, 68)**. The Labour government got round to announcing a large public works policy in the middle of its life, but little had been achieved before its demise, and it is apparent that there was thin enthusiasm for it. Snowden disarmingly told the House of Commons when announcing the plan: 'You are never going to settle the unemployed problem, you are never going to mitigate it to any extent, by making work' **(71)**.

Given the way governments went about the task this was quite likely. Ministers were very unwilling to draw up public works plans themselves; they preferred to urge local authorities to provide relief works and offered to meet some of the costs. Too often the areas most in need of relief were run by financially hard-pressed authorities, unable to find their share of the money. Moreover in the early 1920s official thinking claimed that public works provided no permanent employment and would in effect only give jobs today at the cost of creating unemployment in the future. As short-term temporary palliatives public works seemed unjustifiable. In any case neither aid for British export industries nor relief works were likely to get much cabinet support when the accepted strategy dictated strict economies in government expenditure pending the expected upswing in private industry **(81)**.

What is surprising is the distinct contrast between the cheap and minimal economic policy governments followed while awaiting recovery, and their more expensive and radical welfare provisions. Without realising at the time the full implications of their actions, governments modified the unemployment insurance scheme and accepted new commitments which were to have a profound effect on the development of British social policy. In the summer of 1920, just before the onset of the depression, Lloyd George's government passed an Unemployment Insurance Act which considerably extended prewar legislation to cover most manual workers while raising the level of benefits. According to Professor Gilbert, the inspiration was not an altruistic desire to fulfil wartime promises to construct a land fit for heroes, but more a hurried gesture of social concern designed to defuse a possible revolution led by discontented workers and ex-servicemen in a period of considerable social unrest. When depression struck at the end of 1920 and unemployment rose, government anxieties increased. Under the terms of the 1920 Act, workers were entitled to draw benefits only if they had paid into the fund the statutory number of contributions. If they had not done so they would be forced to rely on the local poor law guardians for relief. Furthermore, qualified workers could draw benefits only for fifteen weeks, after which they too would have to turn to the poor law. The heavy demand on local resources caused by high unemployment was unacceptable to the guardians, but it was also intolerable to most working people, who were repelled by the stigma of pauperism so carefully fostered by poor law authorities in the nineteenth century. Would the discontented masses of the unemployed not prove a potent source of social unrest and perhaps of revolution? Ministers were alarmed. Agitation must be pacified and poor law authorities protected. To do so meant amending the terms of the Unemployment Insurance Act.

To begin with the number of contributions which entitled a worker to claim from the insurance fund was reduced, thus increasing the number of legitimate claimants. But more seriously the number of weeks during which an unemployed worker might claim benefit was changed.

From 1921 workers who had exhausted their rightful claims could, after a while, if still unemployed, claim more weeks 'uncovenanted extended benefit'. The Labour government ended the gap between the periods of benefit. Here was a new principle, the idea not of insurance, but of indefinite maintenance. Also in 1921 another new principle was accepted, that benefits should take some account of family needs: the unemployed could claim dependants' allowances. These modifications at a time of high unemployment put an unbearable strain on the mathematics of insurance. The scheme introduced in 1920 was supposed to be actuarially sound; benefits should be balanced by contributions. That its authors assumed an average unemployment rate of 5.32 per cent was unfortunate. It had been designed to cope with temporary short-term cyclical unemployment and could not, especially in its modified form, handle the burden of persistent depression. The unemployment insurance fund was soon hopelessly in debt, and governments reluctant to spend money on economic recovery were forced to raise loans to feed the voracious appetite of their welfare commitments. The state had accepted a major responsibility which later governments were to find increasingly difficult to handle (60, 65, 67).

Heavy expenditure on mere maintenance and a reluctance to provide work for the unemployed struck some observers as bizarre priorities even if the former was in the short term thought to be cheaper. With the depression dragging on criticisms mounted; government policies and established economic theories were increasingly subjected to searching review. A debate began which was in time to shake the pillars of orthodoxy.

One reasonably coherent alternative strategy was put forward by people who could be described as imperial visionaries. Organised pressure groups inside and outside parliament found a few keen ministerial allies in the early 1920s. Leo Amery was the outstanding enthusiast, as an under-secretary and later as a member of the cabinet. Imperial visionaries were among the first to criticise orthodox policy because many of them had been predicting economic depression since rallied to the cause by Joseph Chamberlain and the Tariff Reform League before the First World War. They disagreed with the official explanation of unemployment; perceptively they argued that British industry was suffering from more than a cyclical depression and was in fact facing a permanent loss of traditional markets overseas and even at home. They attacked the heart of orthodox liberal economic thinking, especially by denying that there was a natural harmony between the interests of the various national economies which made up the international economy: instead there was competition, in competition there were victors, and the unemployed were the casualties. As a remedy the state should so direct private enterprise as to weld the British Empire into a much more economically self-sufficient unit disentangled from the international economy. Tariff barriers with imperial preferences, directed emigration and state investment in the empire would develop its resources, enabling it to supply the food and raw materials needed by Britain while absorbing the bulk of Britain's industrial products. The natural harmony thought to exist between the parts of the empire would guarantee prosperity and full employment at home.

While many cabinet ministers in the early 1920s paid lip service to the idea of increasing empire trade, the visionaries had only a limited influence over government policy. The financial assistance given by the Empire Settlement Act of 1922 steered many British emigrants into the Empire and away from the United States, and a few grants and loans were screwed out of the Treasury to finance colonial development schemes in Africa. However, Amery regarded such measures as merely the start of a long-term strategy of empire development, whereas most ministers saw them as short-term relief measures, shovelling out surplus labour or giving a little help to British exports to the colonies. The striking failure of the visionaries lay in their inability to persuade the nation to abandon free trade. When Baldwin did go to the polls in 1923 on a tariff reform programme he specifically excluded taxing imports of foreign food. Without such tariffs there was no chance of binding the empire into a unit. His electoral defeat in any case confirmed the survival of free trade and the defeat of the imperial visionaries for the rest of the decade [doc. 21]. Because tariffs were expected to lead to a rise in the cost of living, it was difficult to persuade the British people and most politicians of the economic wisdom of opting out of foreign markets and concentrating on the empire (62, 63, 64, 93).

It is significant that another group of critics of orthodox policy also advocated greater state activity as a solution. While most of them accepted a trade cycle explanation of the depression and failed to see the structural problems of British industry, they rejected the orthodox deduction that governments should primarily sit back and expect inevitable recovery, like true believers awaiting the Second Coming. Drawing on some radical ideas expounded before the war, heretics began to explore those concepts of state economic management which have largely governed economic policy since the Second World War. The essential idea was that the state could increase employment by raising the level of demand and so push the economy into a cyclical recovery;

in contrast with orthodox plans, they emphasised policies of reflation not deflation, and the raising of home demand not the restoration of overseas markets.

One school of thought took up the idea of countercyclical public works. The Labour Party had argued in 1918 that 'the Government can, if it chooses, arrange the public works and the orders of National Departments and Local Authorities in such a way as to maintain the aggregate demand for labour in the whole kingdom (including that of capitalist employers) approximately at a uniform level from year to year'. This plan to iron out the fluctuations in the trade cycle by state activity was incorporated in later Labour party statements (72). It was not apparent where the money was to come from to finance such a programme in a period of depression when the government lacked surplus funds, and this explains its rejection by Labour when in office in 1924.

Rivalling it on the left of the Labour party and among some radical Liberals was an underconsumptionist interpretation of the depression. The economist John Hobson described how capitalism put too much of its profits into new investment and distributed too little as wages: the result was low mass purchasing power, underconsumption of industrial products and economic depression. The answer, dear to the hearts of many progressives in Britain, was to raise mass demand through state encouragement for trade unions, an increase in wages and better welfare benefits (86).

Another substantial and influential break with old assumptions was made by critics who focused on the damaging effects of the government's own monetary and fiscal policies as an explanation of the intensity and persistence of the depression in Britain. Although his major text, *The General Theory of Employment, Interest and Money*, was not published until 1936, John Maynard Keynes took some steps towards it in his criticisms of orthodox monetary policy in the early 1920s. In his *Tract on Monetary Reform* (1923) and in *The Economic Consequences of Mr Churchill* (1925), he claimed that the deflationary policies required by a return to the gold standard reduced wages and business confidence and increased unemployment (77, 100). Keynes was by no means alone in these criticisms, and by the mid-1920s plans to expand credit and increase government expenditure and so reflate the economy as a solution to unemployment became more widespread. These ideas can be traced for example in the thinking of the radical wing of the Liberal party under Lloyd George in the mid-1920s, and in the *Revolution by Reason* programme advocated in 1925 by Oswald

Mosley and John Strachey, at that time members of the Independent Labour Party (**77, 95, 107**).

By 1925 radical criticisms of official orthodox policy were being expressed from a number of angles. The division did not necessarily follow party distinctions. Orthodoxy had its defenders among Liberals and Labour supporters as well as among the predominant Tories. Critics could be found as maverick groups of politicians in all parties and among the non-aligned. It is also clear that in 1925 most observers still accepted the government's contention that unemployment was temporary and that orthodox policies would soon bring release. Would such a revival take place and the critics be confounded?

1925–1931

In this second period the critics were not silenced. During the years of Baldwin's government (1924–9), there was a real economic boom overseas, especially in the United States, but unemployment in Britain remained stubbornly around 10 per cent. No recovery had taken place before world depression blew in from overseas and devastated the British economy and the second Labour government (1929–31). The earlier official contention that Britain was suffering from a temporary cyclical depression soluble by traditional means seemed increasingly untenable. To a number of observers, Britain's industrial problems now seemed structural; they might even have been exacerbated by the policies of government. Radical alternatives were essential.

During these years the imperial visionaries maintained their campaign for an imperial tariff system, Empire development and Empire unity. As Secretary of State for the Colonies and for the Dominions between 1924 and 1929, Amery was in a position to press their case on the cabinet. In the ebullient shape of J.H. Thomas, Labour also had a cabinet minister susceptible to the appeal of Empire. As the economic situation worsened a number of politicians such as Neville Chamberlain and Cunliffe-Lister campaigned more actively for at least some of the visionaries' causes. The Empire Industries Association with 200 MPs among its supporters publicised the case, and after his loss of office in 1929 Amery joined Lord Melchett, chairman of ICI, in the formation of a research and propaganda body called the Empire Economic Union (**93**). The most spectacular new force was Lord Beaverbrook's campaign for Empire Free Trade, which also began in 1929. The crusader knight, who still decorates the front page of the *Daily Express*, symbolized the cause. Beaverbrook like Amery wanted to push Baldwin beyond vague sympathy for tariffs and Empire unity into a detailed pledge that the next Conservative government would introduce full tariff protection, including duties on foreign food imports. Baldwin was a heavy boulder to roll. What Amery described as Baldwin's 'molluscous inertia' covered a careful even cunning technique of keeping united behind his leadership a Conservative party which was still hesitant and divided on the issue. In February 1930 the frustrated Beaverbrook for a while joined his fellow press baron, Rothermere, and launched an independent United Empire Party committed to full tariff protection. The party made a reasonable showing in by-elections, but it took the additional persuasion of Neville Chamberlain, plus probably the deteriorating economic position, to wring a pledge from Baldwin in March 1931 committing the Conservative party to tariffs and imperial preferences **(104, 109)**.

There is a revealing contrast between the vigour of the imperial visionaries crusade after 1925 and the paucity of their legislative and administrative achievements by 1931. Most successful had been Amery's work at the Colonial and Dominions Offices. His pressure led to the creation in 1926 of the Empire Marketing Board, which was designed to encourage empire sales in Britain by research, publicity and marketing work. Emigration to Empire countries was still being assisted. Amery had helped improve the colonial services which administered and developed the colonial empire, encouraged scientific research into problems of empire economic production, and squeezed a little more financial help for African colonies out of the Treasury. His main success was to commit the government to supplying £1 million a year to a fund which would finance economic development projects in the colonies and thus stimulate British exports and relieve unemployment. His Bill was endorsed by the Labour government and passed as the Colonial Development Act in 1929. But for Amery these years in office were largely wasted years; his memoirs are a record of frustration. Conflicts with Churchill, the Chancellor of the Exchequer, were frequent and bitter, and despair with Baldwin wearying. The Conservative government ended with scant success for the imperial visionaries' cause. And then with Labour in power, even when economic conditions deteriorated and the balance of trade and the strength of sterling decayed, free trade remained enthroned **(62, 63, 64, 93)**.

The basic arguments of the imperial visionaries had altered little over the years and by 1931 they were sounding a trifle hoarse from repetition. The intellectual excitement in the debate provoked by high unemployment was generated by those economic radicals who advocated techniques of state management of the domestic economy. As part of his attempt to revive a flagging Liberal party with intelligent practical policies, Lloyd George organised and financed the Liberal Industrial Inquiry (not Enquiry lest its initial letters arouse ribaldry). Among its members was Keynes, and his influence can be detected in the unorthodox economic and financial measures proposed in its report, *Britain's Industrial Future*, published in 1928. As well as long-term plans for dealing with the structural problem from which they now saw Britain mainly suffered, the Liberals advocated a public works programme as a short-term emergency scheme. This was further expounded in perhaps the most remarkable political document issued to the public between the wars: a 64-page pamphlet published as the Liberal party's manifesto for the 1929 general election and boldly entitled *We Can Conquer Unemployment*.

Although big public works programmes had been suggested in the past, much was new about this proposal. Most of the plans for road-building, house-building, telephone and electricity development and so on had been worked out in detail, and strikingly the bulk of them were to be crammed into two energetic years. Calculations were made of the amount of employment which would be created, and a brief mention was made of what would later be defined as the multiplier effect, the additional employment created by the prosperity of re-employed workers. But most significantly the financing of the scheme was carefully described. There was no attempt to squeeze the programme into the confines of a balanced budget. The £300 million it might cost would be borrowed by the government and not raised as taxes. As well as showing that the interest on this new debt could easily be met, the plan rejected the idea that the capital required was not available. The money that the state should collect and invest was at present being wasted on doles to the unemployed, or was being invested less beneficially abroad, or, most importantly, was simply lying idle. It was claimed that analysis of bank deposits showed that money was not fully employed, as orthodoxy believed, and the state could therefore borrow and invest it without causing inflation and without taking capital from the hands of private businessmen, as orthodoxy feared (**89, 95**).

Moreover, it seemed to Keynes and a fellow economist, Hubert Henderson, when defending the new proposals that these idle savings also helped explain the cause of the depression. Unemployment rose when demand was low, and domestic demand was low because a central assumption of orthodox thinking was quite wrong: savings, which took demand out of the economy, were not always turned into investments, which put demand back in the form of wages and orders for industrial goods. This was not just an interesting academic observation for it

59

justified and encouraged a practical government policy: government borrowing and expenditure was a way of balancing savings and investment and of securing full employment. This was another step towards *The General Theory* (87) [doc. 22].

The Liberal schemes quite overshadowed the official Labour platform. The party's manifesto of 1928, *Labour and the Nation*, still thought of public works as essentially countercyclical and like the party's reply to Lloyd George in 1929, *How to Conquer Unemployment* (88), it was disturbingly vague on how a Labour government would finance the big public works it proposed to sponsor. Radical plans were viewed suspiciously by the party leadership. In *The Living Wage* (1926), the Independent Labour Party adopted Hobson's underconsumptionist thesis as an explanation of unemployment and recommended a minimum wage standard, family allowances and a state-controlled credit system as a way of increasing demand on the home market (83) [doc. 23]. The plans were condemned by MacDonald as 'flashy futilities'. The proposals drawn up by Oswald Mosley in 1930 when a junior minister in the Labour government received little more sympathy from the party's leaders. Just like the Liberals, Mosley realised that a long-term reconstruction plan needed to be assisted by short-term emergency action to reduce unemployment at once. He too urged a more generous credit policy and large public works directed by the state and financed by loans to stimulate that home market to which many economic radicals looked for recovery: a revival of exports on the old scale was not to be expected. When his plans were rejected and he resigned in May 1930, Mosley partially modified his ideas. By October 1930 he was taking a leaf from the imperial visionaries and advocating, in addition, special economic relations with the Empire to provide Britain with a protected market for her remaining export trade (79, 103, 107).

This amendment indicates some of the overlap between the critics of established policy. The views of Ernest Bevin, General Secretary of the Transport and General Workers' Union, also show this. In 1929 he was appointed to the Macmillan Committee on Finance and Industry. This committee, which also included Keynes, subjected defenders of orthodox financial policy to many unhappy hours of cross-examination and concluded in its report in 1931 that a managed monetary system and a more flexible credit policy were needed to ease the depression (92). The investigation confirmed Bevin in his belief that orthodox policy was responsible for persistent unemployment. In an addendum to the report he joined Keynes in recommending large public works as a way of relieving the immediate crisis, but he went on to propose, as Mosley had done earlier, the abandoning of the gold standard to allow for devaluation. However, Bevin was also a member of the TUC Economic Committee which in 1930 delighted imperial visionaries like Amery and Beaverbrook by recommending the formation of a more self-sufficient economic bloc out of the Empire **(94)**.

Although the economic radicals disagreed deeply with each other on many points, uniting them was the conviction that governments could and should create employment by intervention in the market. Many were prepared to see changes in established political and administrative practices to achieve those ends. Governments ought to be better equipped to handle economic affairs. This might mean altering the size of the cabinet, creating new government departments and appointing professional economists and others as an economic general staff to plan, give advice and collect information. The traditional rights of local authorities might have to be overridden, and even parliament might have to entrust special powers to the executive. Unemployment was often likened to an emergency which like war justified extraordinary measures.

Little of this was acceptable to the governments of Baldwin and MacDonald. What is distinctive about this period is a stubborn adherence to earlier policy even when its operations failed to bring relief and the depression was seen to be more than temporary. In the face of persistent and then worsening unemployment, ministers deviated little from the strategy pursued up to 1925. It was symptomatic of these years that the unimaginative Conservative election slogan in 1929 was 'Safety First'. Labour's policies were equally unexciting. The government's minority position does not explain their timidity: their Liberal allies were prepared for more radical action. As in 1924, Labour leaders could see no permanent solution to the problem but an ill-defined socialism which could be built only on the basis of a restored and prosperous capitalism. Capitalist orthodoxy seemed to them to promise such a recovery. In general, ministers still awaited a cyclical revival of trade.

This meant they still expected a recovery to come primarily through the operations of private enterprise in the free market and not by vigorous state action. Radical plans for administrative and political reform were therefore ignored. Although Baldwin honestly believed that industrial reorganisation and peaceful industrial relations were essential for prosperity, he confessed in 1925: 'It is little that the Government can do: these reforms, these revolutions, must come from the people themselves' **(104)**. The head of the Civil Service told Baldwin in 1929 that to enforce the Liberal plans to solve unemployment would require a Mussolini regime, substituting autocracy for parliamentary government. Baldwin's government set up a Committee of Civil Research and MacDonald formed an Economic Advisory Council, but apart from small-scale investigations and some agreeable academic discussions these talking shops contributed little to government action. In spite of MacDonald's earlier bold plans to create an economic general staff, when in office he merely appointed J.H. Thomas and three comrades, including Mosley, as ministers 'with special responsibilities for unemployment'. But without effective authority over other departments, subordinated in practice to Snowden, the Chancellor, and faced by rising unemployment, Thomas was left in frustration to find what solace he could in drink (**70, 79, 101, 103**).

Assuming that economic recovery would be essentially cyclical, these governments were unable to shake off a preoccupation with exports. Given that Britain needed to export in order to pay for essential imports of food and raw materials and that the bulk of the unemployed had been engaged in the export trades, this concern was understandable. What was not considered was whether the extent of foreign competition, and after 1929 the depression in world markets, would allow exports to recover sufficiently to provide work for all the workless in these industries.

Partly because of this concern with overseas markets, governments continued to seek a settlement of remaining international disputes. The late 1920s were optimistic years, with Germany joining the League of Nations, the powers agreeing to outlaw war by the Kellogg-Briand Pact, diplomatic relations being restored between Britain and Russia and a new settlement of the reparations problem being made. A World Economic Conference in 1927 passed resolutions in favour of greater liberty of trade. This climate promised to restore the international economic system in which Britain's exports might revive. Few ministers contemplated abandoning free trade policy, and many of those who did were restrained by the evident electoral unpopularity of duties on food imports. The Conservatives imposed a few tariffs on a handful of luxury imports, and some minor but vulnerable British industries were protected by the Safeguarding of Industries Acts. But Baldwin eventually decided against a plan to protect the iron and steel industry (**104**), and the dogmatic free-trader Snowden abandoned most existing duties in 1930. Britain entered the whirlpool of the world depression still pledged to free trade and unprotected against the imports which collapsing foreign prices encouraged. Equally, British governments faithfully stuck to the gold standard as part of their commitment to the international economic order. The sacrifices already made, not least by the unemployed, in restoring 'sound currency' were used to justify an adherence to this restrictive monetary policy even when its expected fruits did not ripen (**16, 69, 75**).

A recovery of exports was still thought to be dependent on stable or preferably reduced prices. Proposals to reflate the economy were condemned as likely to cause damaging inflation. Although it can now be seen that wage cuts would reduce home demand, most politicians and many economists believed that 'wage flexibility', by which they meant reductions, would help exports. Baldwin was reported as saying in July 1925: 'All the workers of this country have got to take reductions in wages to help put industry on its feet' **(104)**. Fortunately for the home market and in spite of the General Strike in 1926, his government could do little to enforce its beliefs and severe wages reductions were mainly confined to the depressed export industries. On the whole wage rates remained stable until 1931 **(2)**.

A strategy which claimed that private enterprise assisted by the gold standard and a regime of low prices would bring economic recovery to Britain continued to affect budgetary policy. It is true that the savage deflationary pressures of the early 1920s were not maintained throughout the decade, but it was still believed that taxes had to be kept down and borrowing avoided so as to reduce industrial costs and leave more money in the pockets of consumers and producers. Chancellors accepted as a consequence that their annual budgets should balance, though there may have been an unreality in the balances achieved since they largely ignored the mounting deficit in the separate account of the Unemployment Insurance Fund. Moreover Churchill's budgets balanced only by cooking the books: raiding the road fund, juggling with the sinking fund, advancing the date for the payment of income tax. On the whole and largely by accident, Churchill's budgets were mildly inflationary, though still an inadequate stimulus to a depressed economy. But the commitment to orthodoxy remained, most vividly demonstrated by Churchill's successor, Snowden, who attacked the budget deficit bequeathed to him with all the fervour of a Puritan divine chastising sin. His 1930 budget raised income tax and some indirect taxes, and in the crisis of 1931, when depression cried out for relief, worse was to come **(2)**.

It also followed that government expenditure had to be tightly restricted. Although both administrations argued that recovery lay through an export revival they were reluctant to spend money to achieve that end. Export credits were continued, but the Trade Facilities Act was allowed to lapse in 1927. Both governments favoured assisting exports to the colonies but only a little financial encouragement was given **(62)**. There was one distinctive Conservative measure: in his 1928 budget Churchill contrived to find the money for a scheme to relieve industry of three-quarters of its rate burden and to give block grants to local authorities instead, calculated to give most money to areas where unemployment was severe. It does not seem to have made a noticeable difference to industrial costs (2, 97, 105). Both governments made much of the acceleration of normal departmental public works they authorised, building roads and extending electricity supplies for example, and of the continued work of the Unemployment Grants Committee. But the scale of the Conservative programme was small and the restrictions imposed by government on the operations of the UGC virtually suppressed the scheme for three years. Labour began more vigorously, announcing extra departmental work, reviving the UGC and creating a new development fund in 1929 to help finance construction schemes on the railways, in the docks and elsewhere; but since the authorised work was to be spread over a number of years its effects on unemployment would be slight (68, 79).

Substantial public expenditure to relieve unemployment was ruled out by both governments; indeed, if anything, the official attitude hardened at a time when many outsiders were seeing more merit in large-scale public works. The fundamental objection was expressed by Churchill in his budget speech in 1929: 'It is orthodox Treasury dogma, steadfastly held, that whatever might be the political or social advantages, very little additional employment can, in fact, and as a general rule be created by State borrowing and expenditure.' Few professional economists would have subscribed to this iron law, but it was the opinion which ruled Treasury thinking when condemning the proposals put forward by radicals such as Lloyd George in 1929 or Mosley in 1930. Baldwin instructed the Civil Service to scrutinise the Liberal plan and took the unusual step of issuing a white paper based on their criticisms (91). Perfectly valid points were made about the practical difficulties obstructing big emergency construction schemes, but the Treasury's objections were also more fundamental. It had been argued earlier in the 1920s that public works merely provided work today which would not therefore be available tomorrow. Now the objection was that government borrowing to finance employment schemes would merely take equivalent resources out of the hands of private industry, thus creating no net increase in employment. This mirage had already been exposed in the Liberal manifesto which pointed out that if this were true about government borrowing and expenditure it must be true of private borrowing and expenditure, in which case no solution to unemployment was possible; in fact, a mere diversion of employment would only take place if all savings were fully invested. This the Treasury continued to insist was the case: there were no idle savings. The only other source for government borrowing would be to prevent loans from going abroad and this would restrict those exports which orthodoxy believed followed them and which the official mind still viewed as the key to salvation [doc. 22]. Similar objections were made against Mosley's proposals: 'The finance of these schemes would not stand a moment's consideration', records Labour's Chancellor (108). Such thinking left governments impotent (68, 81).

There were only a few signs that governments in this period recognised the need to deal with the structural problem at the root of continuing unemployment. Both administrations included in their plans for an export recovery certain proposals to revitalise the staple industries. The aim was to make them more successful by rationalisation schemes which would encourage amalgamations and the modernisation of production methods while reducing wasteful competition by closing the less efficient units. With Baldwin's support, the Bank of England helped create the Lancashire Cotton Corporation in 1929 which set about reducing the size and increasing the efficiency of the industry. In the following year the Bank of England formed the Bankers' Industrial Development Corporation which provided the financial backing for the National Shipbuilders Security Ltd. to perform similar functions, buying up and closing surplus shipyards [doc. 24]. A Labour government investigation of the cotton industry reported in 1930 in favour of more substantial reductions in capacity, and one section of the Coal Mines Act of 1930, although abortive in practice, was supposed to encourage amalgamations and the closure of inefficient pits. A consequence of this policy was apparent even to its supporters. While closures and modernisation might conceivably deal with the economic problem of falling exports, they did not help the social problem of unemployment since as a result less labour was needed (12, 104).

One government scheme claimed to offer special help for the unemployed in the distressed areas. The Industrial Transference Board was appointed in 1928 to help migration out of South Wales, the North East and Scotland of workers, especially miners, for whom unemployment seemed permanent. The board was simply to coordinate and encourage the activities of employment exchanges, training centres and the Overseas Settlement Office, and to give some financial help to migrants. Though the transference scheme was continued right through the 1930s, one obstacle never tackled was the pockets of unemployment even in the more prosperous areas. Without a large expansion of employment opportunities in the South and East there would be no migration from the North and Wales on the scale required to solve the problem, even if such movement were socially desirable. The policy was symptomatic of the thinking of the 1920s which assumed labour was more mobile than capital. Workers should move to find jobs:

industry should not be compelled to move to areas of high unemployment (2, 68) [doc. 25].

While governments were still reluctant to spend money on the provision of work, their commitment to maintaining the unemployed with unemployment insurance plunged them into great financial difficulties and finally into crisis. The system of providing the workless from insured trades with weekly benefits for the whole period of their unemployment was confirmed in a new Insurance Act in 1927. Workers exhausting legitimate insurance claims could still draw 'transitional benefits' to keep them off poor relief. The only qualification for this was that the applicant must show he was 'genuinely seeking work'. This generosity was based on the quite erroneous assumption that unemployment would soon decline to 6 per cent. Worsening unemployment increased the number of claims and the debt of the unemployment insurance fund. These also rose substantially when the Labour government abolished the 'genuinely seeking work' clause in 1930, and so made claims to transitional benefit a right which employment exchanges could challenge only with difficulty. But the major significance of the 1930 Act was that the whole cost of transitional benefits was taken from the account of the unemployment insurance fund and made a burden on the Treasury's annual budget. In the year ending March 1931 transitional benefits cost the taxpayer nearly £20 million. While easing a little the pressure on the unemployment insurance fund, the transfer unwittingly added to the problems which brought the Labour government to ruin in August 1931 (67).

Two especially grave developments troubled Britain by the summer of 1931. First, there was a monetary problem. Since the First World War British governments had struggled to revive and support the gold standard as part of an international system in which British industry as well as British finance was expected to flourish. But by 1930, battered by the world depression, Canada, Australia, New Zealand and six Latin American countries had already abandoned gold. During the summer of 1931 there was a decline of confidence in the pound and a drain of gold overseas, and this threatened Britain's adherence to the gold standard. An adverse balance of payments then caused fresh alarm but this was intensified by a banking crisis which spread from Austria. Concern turned to panic when it was seen that the forthcoming government budget would be hopelessly unbalanced. This links with the second grave development, a rise in unemployment to over 2½ million when British exports slumped. Serious though this increase was it provoked a major crisis only because it increased the debt of the unemployment insurance fund and the burden of transitional benefits on the budget at a time when government revenues from taxation were falling. The budget would not balance.

The orthodox policy which dominated everything was to protect the gold standard: abandonment or devaluation were not considered by the authorities. To create confidence in the pound so as to protect Britain's gold reserves it was assumed that the government must prove it was creditworthy by balancing the budget. Snowden refused to increase direct taxation or suspend the sinking fund, and this meant that government expenditure had to be savagely cut. Searching for economies the government passed the Anomalies Act, which excluded certain workers, especially married women, from claiming unemployment benefit. It also appointed a Committee on National Expenditure under Sir George May to propose cuts in government spending sufficient to balance the budget. The committee's report in July 1931 portrayed such a serious imbalance as to shatter overseas confidence in the pound. Foreign bankers to whom the government turned for credits requested reductions in government expenditure before loans would be made. The cabinet was obliged to discuss cuts in public sector pay, in the road-building programme and, most importantly, in unemployment benefits. The May Committee, Snowden and foreign bankers insisted upon this last item. So too did the Conservative leaders, busily twisting the knife in Labour's side. It is clear that the demand for cuts was the consensus at home and abroad. The heretical alternatives of devaluation or revenue tariffs discussed by Keynes, the TUC and a few others were ignored. The cabinet too accepted the need to balance the budget. However, in the end, nearly half the ministers rebelled at the proposal that a Labour government should be responsible for a 10 per cent cut in unemployment benefits and this split ended Labour's rule. On 24 August 1931 MacDonald formed a National government. Transfixed by orthodox assumptions, the Labour government could only squirm helplessly. It had been unable to prevent a rise in unemployment and now could not even protect the doles of those out of work (11, 67, 69, 79).

1931–1939

In comparison with its predecessors the National government under MacDonald (1931–5), Baldwin (1935–7) and Chamberlain (1937–40) appears distinctly unorthodox. The crisis which swept away the Labour government seems to have shaken some of the rigidity out of official thinking. Recent studies, for example, have shown the development of closer and more sympathetic contacts between some of the radical economists and the new generation of top civil servants at the Treasury. It is to this decade especially that we can trace back the origins of the Keynesian revolution in official thinking and government policy (69, 70). But close examination also shows that before the Second World War the intellectual conversion was seriously incomplete. The dead-weight of orthodox ideas and policies continued to prevent more effective responses to the persistent problem of unemployment. It is also apparent that some of the more radical innovations of the National government were forced on it by circumstances beyond its control.

The orthodox instincts of the new government were seen at once. It took as its first task the defence of the pound and the gold standard. In order to raise foreign loans to protect sterling it pressed on where Labour drew back and imposed economies in government expenditure. To balance the budget in September, Snowden, still Chancellor, cut the pay of teachers, the police, the armed forces and other public servants, and imposed the 10 per cent reduction in unemployment benefit. Moreover, standard benefits were henceforth to be paid for a maximum of twenty-six weeks after which additional benefits, now called 'transitional payments', would be allowed only after a family means test. To add insult to injury, the means test would be operated by the same local authorities which since 1930 had been administering the poor law, the Public Assistance Committees. Ironically even before this package was passed the drain on gold had turned to a flood and the government had to abandon the gold standard on 21 September. The struggle to revive and preserve the self-regulating exchange system which had dominated government policy since 1919 was over (11, 67).

This catastrophe forced the dismayed authorities into the monetary management they had tried to avoid. In April 1932 the Exchange Equalisation Account was formed, which by buying and selling in the foreign exchange market was able to maintain the reasonably stable sterling exchange rate British exports needed. At the same time, however, it prevented movements of foreign funds into and out of the country from upsetting the level of domestic credit. This separation of internal financial affairs from external factors had been proposed by radical monetarists like Keynes, but it was the failure of the country to stay on the gold standard which forced the government to accept it. Henceforth the state had a new role as monetary manager (2, 69).

The advantages of the new system were immediately realised by the more perceptive Treasury officials. So long as Britain was bound to the gold standard and needed to attract foreign funds to maintain the parity of sterling, the bank rate had stayed high. Now, insulated from the outside world by the Exchange Equalisation Account, the rate could be brought down. From June 1932 until the end of the decade it was 2 per cent. It used to be thought that this cheap money policy aimed simply to deter imports of 'hot money' from abroad which would be attracted by a higher rate and also to help the government raise a huge conversion loan. A lower bank rate brought other interest rates down and enabled the government to pay off a 5 per cent war loan with a 3½ per cent conversion loan, so reducing annual interest payments and making it easier to balance the budget (2, 76). The government did have these strictly orthodox objectives in mind but we now know they were also persuaded to reduce the bank rate by Treasury officials who saw a cheap money policy as a way of stimulating domestic investment. Radical thinkers had been suggesting for some time that easier credit would encourage economic recovery. Freed at last from the restrictions of the gold standard policy, the Treasury was prepared to adopt this strategy (69).

Unfortunately the opportunities offered by the new monetary policy were incompletely recognised. By the end of the 1920s many radicals were arguing that in a period of acute economic gloom it was not enough to enable private enterprise to borrow money more cheaply. Valuable though this was, it was imperative that the government should also set the economy on the upturn and provide an example to businessmen by its own borrowing and expenditure. A reflationary fiscal policy was needed: orthodox balanced budgets should be abandoned. Against such heresies as deficit-financing and large-scale public works the National government for the most part set its face. Some Treasury officials came to see merit in the proposals, but only when war threatened and rearmament became unavoidable from 1936 did the government actually borrow and spend large amounts of money. In fact, their actions then unwittingly halted the recession becoming apparent late in 1937. Otherwise ministers assumed that a cheap money policy would be sufficient to encourage private enterprise to lead the country along the path of natural economic recovery.

Accordingly government fiscal policy did little to help. Budgets generated surpluses in most years and tended to be deflationary even in the depths of the depression. It was typical of the orthodox thinking which persisted that unemployment benefit was cut in 1931 and not restored until economic conditions had improved in 1934. Only a few central government measures were designed directly to provide work for the workless, and they were piecemeal and small in scale: guaranteeing interest payments for railway construction work and London transport developments, providing a loan to restart construction of the *Queen Mary*, abandoned half-built two years before, and giving more loans to encourage tramp-shipping owners to place new orders under a 'scrap and build' scheme. The government tried to claim credit for such measures at the general election in 1935, but they did not show much of an advance on government proposals in the 1920s (2, 12, 84).

When the government did make a significant innovation in employment policy it was largely in response to public pressure. The world depression hit regions in the North and Wales with exceptional severity. Official and unofficial reports emphasised the structural nature of their difficulties, local MPs and *The Times* pressed for action, agitation by the unemployed kept the issue before the public. The government's reluctant response was the Special Areas Act of 1934. This recognised the problems of particular districts in Southern Scotland, the North East, West Cumberland and South Wales. However the two commissioners appointed were empowered to spend a mere £2 million a year, mainly helping local authorities carry out amenity schemes, encouraging land settlement and trying to persuade firms to move into the areas. After more public agitation and criticisms of the original Act, not least by one of the commissioners, its powers were widened by legislation in 1936 and 1937 to enable the Treasury to give financial help to companies prepared to invest in distressed areas, and additional funds were made available [doc. 26].

The results remained fairly modest. By the end of 1938 the commissioners were committed to spending only £17 million. A number of firms had been induced to move into the regions and a handful of gleaming new trading estates had been built, as in Team Valley near Gateshead. For the fortunate individuals re-employed and for some local communities this special assistance was a blessing, but in all probably less than 50,000 new jobs were created in areas where over 350,000 were registered as unemployed in January 1935. Nevertheless it was a more imaginative method of directly helping the unemployed. The government abandoned the argument of the Industrial Transference Board whose plans to help migration were quite evidently inadequate, and began to encourage capital to move to labour. It admitted that unemployment had structural and therefore regional characteristics, and it accepted the need for a constructive regional aid policy. Henceforth such schemes would be part of all future government economic policies (2, 12).

The recovery of British exports which the British government obviously still desired led ministers to press even more for the rationalisation of the staple export trades in order to improve their international competitiveness. The Finance Act of 1935, for example, gave tax relief to industries whose plans for reorganisation would shed excess capacity. But this carrot was tempered by the novel application of the stick: there was an extra emphasis on state compulsion. The iron and steel industry was given tariff protection only on the understanding that reorganisation took place; similarly an Act in 1936 forced the cotton industry to scrap excess spinning capacity, and legislation in 1939 laid down compulsory minimum prices for cotton goods. Attempts to force amalgamations and closures in the coal industry proved more difficult: a new Act in 1938 attempted to tighten up the process. This reorganisation of the staple industries was important in the government's plans for export recovery, but since the main effect was to reduce their size, it inevitably created redundancies not jobs (12).

Since the National government was dominated by the Conservatives it was predictable that the radical policy it embraced most enthusiastically was the introduction of tariff barriers to protect the home market. The crisis of 1931 provided the opportunity which zealots like Neville Chamberlain desired. The flood of foreign imports into Britain, the adverse balance of payments and the attraction of tariffs as a source of extra government revenue to meet budgetary needs were persuasive arguments. The electorate responded by returning massive numbers of avowed protectionists in the general election in October 1931, and most of those ministers who had been traditionally staunch free traders bowed to the inevitable. The punitive duties imposed as an emergency measure in 1931 and then the Import Duties Act of 1932 ended the era of free trade (63).

Abandoning the gold standard and imposing tariff protection in 1931–2 was the National government's contribution to the destruction of that international economic order whose defence previous British governments had held as central to their strategy for economic recovery. Little could be done to prevent this demolition. In the world depression beginning in 1929, the national incomes of the industrial countries fell severely, unemployment soared and world trade slumped. Nations sought individual survival in self-protection, by abandoning the gold standard, by exchange controls and by tariff barriers. Control over large home markets or the subordination of neighbouring satellite economies enabled some industrial nations, including the United States, Russia, Germany and Japan, to abandon the international system in favour of the more self-sufficient economic blocs they dominated. In some respects Britain followed suit: the government exercised much tighter control over the export of capital, most of the overseas investment allowed being directed into the Empire. Moreover, an Imperial conference at Ottawa in 1932 concluded with preferential tariff arrangements between Britain and the rest of the British Empire.

Furthermore, virtually the whole of the Empire plus a number of other foreign countries formed a sterling area, linking their currencies to the pound when Britain left the gold standard (12, 63).

But it is apparent that after the first shock of 1931–2, the National government was not content to commit British fortunes to an Empire or sterling bloc. It sought to revive some of its earlier international ties. In 1933 MacDonald presided over a World Economic Conference in London designed to stabilise exchange rates and liberalise trade by international cooperation. However, the forces of economic nationalism prevented delegates from reaching agreement. As A.J.P. Taylor observed, the meeting was held in the Geological Museum at South Kensington where principles like free trade could be suitably preserved as fossils from the past (16). What the British government did later achieve with the aim of encouraging overseas trade were some important special arrangements: a monetary agreement with France and the United States in 1936, and a total of twenty bilateral trade agreements with foreign countries between 1933 and 1938 (12, 64).

Another change of significance for the future was made in government welfare policy which had already seen so many radical departures since the end of the First World War. As Chancellor of the Exchequer in 1932, Chamberlain was worried by the continuation of an unemployment insurance scheme which failed to distinguish between short-term and long-term unemployment and which under the transitional payments schemes left the assessment and expenditure of central government money to the discretion of local Public Assistance Committees. The consequent lack of uniformity upset his bureaucratic mind, especially when some committees paid 'excessive' benefits. Two authorities, Rotherham and Co. Durham were found guilty of overgenerosity and were replaced by Ministry of Labour commissioners. Supported by the findings of a Royal Commission on Unemployment Insurance (85), Chamberlain's musings led in time to the Unemployment Act of 1934. Part I of the Act restored an actuarially balanced contributory insurance scheme for the short-term unemployed to be operated by the Unemployment Insurance Statutory Committee. It prospered so well that it was able to increase dependants' allowances in 1936 and 1938.

Part II was more novel. A central government Unemployment Assistance Board was formed which was to pay means-tested benefits through its agents in local offices to the non-insured unemployed and to the long-term insured unemployed who had exhausted their insurance rights after claiming benefit for twenty-six weeks. The board therefore replaced the system under which the granting of poor relief and transitional payments to the unemployed had been the responsibility of the Public Assistance Committees of the local authorities. Uproar among the unemployed and their sympathisers against the proposed scales of benefit delayed the introduction of the new scheme until 1937. But in spite of this inauspicious beginning, the Act was a model for later developments in social policy. Since the Second World War, the welfare state has combined contributory, national insurance schemes with non-contributory, means-tested, state-controlled and taxpayer-financed additional help known as national assistance or later as supplementary benefits **(60, 65, 67)** **[doc. 27]**.

How far did the policies of the National government satisfy the economic radicals? It might seem that the early actions of the National government would delight imperial visionaries like Amery. Tariffs in 1931–2 made possible the negotiation of preferential agreements with the dominions at Ottawa and these did increase the flow of trade within the Empire. But even in 1932, Amery regretted the failure of the government to aim at a reflationary monetary policy for the British Empire as a unit as a way of inducing trade expansion between its parts. His fears that the National government was not making the most of its imperial opportunities were increased, first, when the Empire Marketing Board was abolished in 1933 as an economy measure and, second, when the bilateral trade agreements the government made with foreign countries showed it was still hankering after an international rather than an imperial basis for British prosperity.

Imperial visionaries felt there was much work to be done. Amery was excluded from the National government, but his books, articles and speeches continued to flow, and with suitable homage the Empire Industries Association celebrated the centenary of the birth of Joseph Chamberlain in 1936 with a new campaign **(82, 93)**. In the 1930s that flawed genius Oswald Mosley also proposed imperial unity as part of the economic programme of his British Union of Fascists, planning for example to suppress India's textile industry to revive the fortunes of Lancashire's ailing export trade **(107)**. At least this scheme had the merit of recognising what the haggling at the Ottawa conference had exposed; the lack of a natural economic harmony between the parts of the British Empire. Imperial economic unity was increasingly anachronistic. India and the dominions defended their own industries against imports of British manufactured goods; even British agriculture demanded protection against some empire products. The flow of migration to the Empire was also reversed in the 1930s, and low prices for food and raw materials did not encourage colonial governments to develop their primary resources. Even in 1938 only 47 per cent of

British exports went to the Empire and only 39 per cent of British imports were supplied by it. The National government did not, and probably could not, do much to satisfy the visions of imperial enthusiasts (63).

Those who advocated the use of monetary and fiscal policies to stimulate the domestic market continued to expound and develop their theories in the 1930s. Indeed the range of converts distinctly widened (74). The disaster of 1931 shook the Labour party out of its intellectual torpor. Between 1931 and 1934 it drew up a new short-term programme for a future Labour government, which in planning to create full employment by a reflationary monetary policy and by a state investment programme to soak up idle savings, clearly owed much to the Liberal party, Keynes and the radicals of the 1920s. Its grasp of the new economics was still a little unsure, and the programme remained a subject of contention within the party, largely because what it offered was not full socialism but state-managed capitalism in a mixed economy (61, 96). It is revealing of the consensus among radicals of all parties that the Labour party's new views were very similar to the ideas expressed by Harold Macmillan, a dissident Tory, in his significantly titled book *The Middle Way*. This was another proposal for a state-managed mixed economy, eschewing both full state control and doctrinaire laissez-faire, and using monetary and fiscal techniques plus minimum wage legislation and generous welfare allowances to raise and sustain the level of demand and therefore of employment (90, 102) [doc. 28]. Lloyd George was also still active in these years. Echoing Roosevelt's innovations in the United States, he launched his New Deal with appropriate theatricals in Bangor in January 1935, brushing up his 1929 plans for a huge reflationary public works scheme (106). Mosley's British Union of Fascists manifesto, *The Greater Britain* (1932), similarly contained a revised version of his earlier plans to raise employment levels (107).

Although unorthodox policy proposals and the economic thinking which lay behind them drew on many sources, many radicals acknowledged their debt to Keynes. His views developed in the early 1930s, and in 1935 he was able to declare with characteristic immodesty that he was writing a book which would 'largely revolutionise the way in which the world thinks about economic problems' (100). This of course was to be *The General Theory of Employment, Interest and Money* (1936). In this he developed his analysis of the forces which set the level of employment in the economy. He showed that employment depended on the amount of money people spent and invested. He described the factors which encouraged consumption and investment, and explained how changes in the level of consumption and investment had cumulative effects through the multiplier on the level of employment. He then demonstrated that there were no automatic self-regulating market forces which would ensure that the amount of spending and investment by millions of individuals in society would necessarily be just enough to provide work for all. This attacked the heart of orthodox classical economics. The natural corollary was that the state should use monetary and fiscal techniques in order to affect the level of consumption and investment and therefore create full employment (80, 81).

Those radicals who desired active state economic management approved of some of the National government's innovations. Some of them like Keynes were members of the government's Committee on Economic Information, which brought them as advisers into touch with Treasury officials. They were delighted to find a more sympathetic consideration of their views than in the past (70). They naturally welcomed the abandonment of the gold standard and the creation of the new system of exchange controls, and regarded the cheap money policy as a valuable measure. But on balance the government was still open to their criticisms. They were frustrated especially by the orthodoxy of the government's fiscal policy and by its continued expectation of a natural economic recovery led by private investment. Lloyd George's New Deal plans, for example, were considered by the cabinet only to be rejected. Other plans for large-scale public works were also ignored. The government seemed complacent, too tolerant of the slow rate of recovery and of the remaining high level of unemployment.

The radicals were equally annoyed by the National government's poor response to the new enthusiasm for state economic planning (74, 81). Conceptually distinct but sometimes linked to ideas of monetary and fiscal management, planning, it was claimed, would increase industrial efficiency and create full employment by state coordination and direction of industrial and financial activities. The scope of planning varied according to the proposer, but there was a consensus which favoured state control of key and ailing industries, state direction of investment to desirable goals and the integration of nationalised industries with a private sector. Several factors encouraged this new vogue: the inspiration of German, Italian and Russian plans, the practical experience by businessmen of the management of big national companies, the seemingly unshiftable problem of the depressed regions and above all the evident failure of unguided capitalism to prevent unemployment. Where the free market had failed, state planning might succeed. Such hopes were expressed by non-party organisations like the Political and Economic Planning group formed in 1931 and the Liberal and Democratic Leadership group which published a detailed scheme, *The Next Five Years*, in 1935. Similar ideas were put forward by Boothby and Macmillan (102). They were especially taken up by the Labour party in a series of policy statements; special attention was paid to the revival of the depressed areas by state-planned investment (61, 96).

It is true that governments did extend their controls and influence over industry and agriculture especially in the 1930s: marketing arrangements for farmers were major innovations. But ministers did not plan an integrated scheme to direct national or even regional economic recovery. There was a typical lack of connection between rationalisation schemes which reduced local employment and the slender efforts made to encourage new investment in depressed areas. Businesses were allowed to follow market forces with the result that most expansion took place elsewhere (2, 53). This failure of the left hand to recognise what the right hand was doing dismayed some observers and was another factor making planning seem essential.

The National government claimed in its manifesto in 1935 that 'under this leadership we have emerged from the depths of depression to a condition of steadily returning prosperity' (84). Ministers were naturally inclined to take the credit for such recovery as did take place in the 1930s. Historians have been reluctant to endorse their claims. Recently the value of the cheap money policy in stimulating a housing boom has been stressed (69), but none of the government's other policies are regarded as really decisive, even though they sometimes deviated from orthodox traditions. Devaluation in 1931 gave only a temporary boost to the economy, tariffs at best protected some industries from greater distress, and imperial preferences diverted rather than increased the flows of Britain's overseas trade. Balanced budgets may have helped business confidence, but until rearmament began government expenditure did little to improve overall employment prospects. Some historians insist that whatever the government did achieve was overshadowed by an unassisted expansion of the home market. They see falling prices, smaller families and rising expectations as primarily responsible for the housing boom and the expansion of consumer goods industries which were the main sources of Britain's economic growth (2, 13). Even this substantial achievement left a grim burden of unemployment and exposed the continued failure of Britain's interwar governments.

Part Three: Assessment

Several points may be made in defence of government policy between the wars. The problem they faced was one of unprecedented severity. Basically what was happening in these twenty years, especially in the 1930s, was the modernisation of the British economy, a substantial shift of resources from the nineteenth-century staple trades into newer industries such as motor-car manufacturing, chemicals, electrical engineering and consumer goods production: these would form the basis of the country's economic growth after the Second World War. The unemployed were to a large extent the victims of this momentous, unplanned, barely recognised transformation. It was not unreasonable for ministers in the early 1920s to be unaware of this and to expect the depression to ease as earlier cyclical downturns had done. Moreover, no sooner had they begun to discern the structural troubles of the economy at the end of the decade than crisis overseas swept Britain into the world depression of the 1930s. Since unemployment was then a problem common to most industrial nations, it seemed obvious to ministers that some general factor, like obstacles to world trade, must be largely responsible for the world's trouble. Hence the continued attention paid by ministers to the condition of Britain's export trade and the desire to resurrect the international economy. Hence British enthusiasm for such a reconstruction during and after the Second World War and their sympathy for the general idea if not the detailed practice of the World Bank, the International Monetary Fund and the General Agreement on Trade and Tariffs. There was wisdom in this: Britain did need to export in order to import the essentials for prosperity: food and raw materials. But such a priority also meant that governments were less aware of Britain's special structural problems, and did far less 'than was necessary to guide the country through its pubescent agonies as it matured into a modernised twentieth-century economy.

It is apparent that when unemployment did become a world problem, most overseas governments stumbled along orthodox trails searching for solutions. There was no shining foreign model of a government dealing effectively *and* humanely with mass unemployment. In the

77

eyes of British ministers the removal of the problem in Nazi Germany and Soviet Russia involved the loss of a good deal more, including civil liberty. For all the bustling activity of Roosevelt's New Deal there remained much that was incoherent, even contradictory, in its conception and operation, and with 13 million Americans out of work in 1933 and still almost 8 million in the best year 1937, it did not seem conspicuously successful (5). More attention might have been paid to economic management in Sweden although historians are now reluctant to claim that radical policy was decisive in promoting Swedish recovery (2, 73).

It would be unwise to assume that the untried radical alternatives proposed at home would have been magic wands to wave unemployment away. Imperial visionaries too easily assumed that the vigorously independent dominions would necessarily fall in with British plans for imperial economic cooperation. Given the limited resources and markets of the Empire it could not have been formed into an entirely self-sufficient bloc supplying all its wants and absorbing all its products as some extremists claimed. Reflationists were also slow to consider whether their plans would increase imports, deter exports and damage the balance of payments. Nor is it entirely certain that the world was waiting for Keynes. The monetary and fiscal solutions he proposed in his 1920s writings and in *The General Theory* might have checked cyclical depression, but it can be argued that he offered no solution to the structural problem which lay at the heart of regional unemployment. Government action to stimulate aggregate demand in the economy might have soaked up the pools of unemployment in the growing areas of the South and East, but it might have still left a severe problem in South Wales or Tyneside unless the demand generated by monetary and fiscal policies either revived existing industries in these areas (which is doubtful) or encouraged the settlement there of new industries. For that to happen government planning and direction of investment would probably be necessary and on this Keynes himself had little to say (18). The most practical programmes for government action were those like Macmillan's *The Middle Way*, which combined state direction of industry with the supporting financial policies for which Keynes's mature work provided the theoretical justification. Such proposals were not fully developed until the late 1930s. In the light of Britain's economic problems in the 1970s it can also be less easily claimed that the new economic thinking of the 1930s produced all the answers.

In the meantime the pressures on governments to keep to orthodoxy were severe. The advice of the entrenched professionals in the Treasury, in the City and from many outside commentators urged allegiance to the old ways, especially in the 1920s. As attempts in 1931 to raise foreign loans to support sterling demonstrated, it was the expectation of influential overseas financiers also. In addition, orthodoxy was demanded by most MPs: the swinging of the Geddes Axe cutting government expenditure in 1921–2 followed one such 'anti-waste' campaign, the formation of the May Committee in 1931 followed another. In such circumstances, a bold rejection of traditional beliefs was made more difficult.

Interwar governments derived some comfort from a consideration of the social consequences of the depression. The world depression of the early 1930s was felt more seriously overseas than in Britain. The volume of unemployment and cuts in income were certainly more severe in the United States. Extensions of Britain's unemployment insurance scheme plus the additional assistance of local welfare and voluntary services did prevent a huge social disaster in this country. Intolerable though the effects of the depression on the unemployed may now seem, ministers had some grounds for feeling relieved that their policies had prevented a more grinding reduction in living standards, a more alarming deterioration in health and more dangerous outbreaks of violence and political militancy.

But when all allowances have been made, these years did bring exceptional hardship to many families. The improvements in living standards and health which nationally were taking place were checked in the worst hit areas. It is simplistic but on the whole legitimate to see Britain, especially in the 1930s, dividing into two nations, a relatively affluent South and East where new industries were settling and expanding, and a more stagnant comparatively declining North and West where old industries struggled. This was a historical change of some size, reversing a nineteenth-century pattern which in the past had brough better employment prospects, higher wages and greater prosperity to places like Tyneside, Lancashire, West Cumberland, the Clyde and South Wales than to areas in the South and East. Governments showed themselves powerless to guide the interwar changes and to eliminate the social hardships they brought.

In the First World War, and later in the Second World War, British governments revealed that they were not incapable of vigorous action to control the economy when military necessity required it. They were strangely reluctant to act with determination in the 'normal' years between the fighting. In a sense, with the important exception of the unemployment insurance scheme, governments never had an unemployment policy. One or two public works schemes were tried with increasing disfavour, but essentially unemployment was regarded as a symptom and not as a problem. Instead of lancing boils, ministers attempted to purify the bloodstream. The cure lay in creating those conditions which were thought to be most conducive to the natural flows of trade. Like mother nature, the economy was expected to operate best when left alone, unsullied by the muddy hand of government intervention. This 'ecological' approach to unemployment encouraged governments to assist what they believed to be normal recuperative market forces. Hence the concern shown throughout these years to leave capital to fructify in the pockets of private enterprise · and to reduce government borrowing and expenditure. This explains the steps taken in the 1920s to restore the gold standard. It lay behind a government willingness in the 1930s to reduce interest rates for private industry while still avoiding state investment. In the 1930s the National government did intervene more consciously in the market with a managed currency and tariffs, but ministers could not shake off the remaining assumption that they could best help recovery and revive employment prospects by facilitating and then awaiting an increase in private business activity. A more direct cure for unemployment, such as advocates of large-scale public works proposed, was thought to obstruct that natural process.

What seems so dismal in the conduct of interwar governments is their refusal to contemplate radical reflationary proposals. They could not be tempted into experiments, although some foreign governments were prepared to try, and coherent alternative strategies had been devised at home. That such experiments might not have proved completely successful in no way explains why governments opted for caution and refused to consider them, even when orthodoxy had been pursued so conscientiously and had failed so conspicuously.

The timidity of ministers was not due to the absence of alternative economic theories but to a failure of political will. Ministers proved themselves inadequate to their tasks. Professor Mowat writes that with the end of Coalition government in 1922, 'the rule of the pygmies, of the "second-class brains" began, to continue until 1940' (11). It is difficult to fault his judgement. We may notice the orthodox advice pressed by Civil Service pundits on ministers responsible for economic matters; what is alarming is how willing ministers were to continue accepting this advice, how unwilling they were to challenge it. It is apparent that the financial and economic difficulties held to be responsible for unemployment were regarded by many interwar politicians as arcane mysteries comprehensible only to the initiated in the Treasury and in the City of London. Churchill had little experience of economic affairs before becoming Chancellor of the Exchequer in 1924, and neither Baldwin nor MacDonald could do more than mouth simple propositions in debates on unemployment. Only a few leading politicians felt themselves fully in command of financial and economic arguments. Of these, some like Snowden and Neville Chamberlain accepted the orthodox theories of their advisers as indisputable truths beyond serious question. Churchill wrote that Snowden and the Treasury 'embraced each other with the fervour of two long-separated kindred lizards' (79). Speaking of credit and currency problems, Snowden told a Labour party conference that 'Parliament is not a competent body to deal with the administration of such highly delicate and intricate matters' (81). This tendency to regard economic and financial policy as scientific answers to technical questions in effect denied the possibility of alternative answers and attempted to push such subjects out of the political debate.

Shackled to orthodoxy in this unquestioning fashion, ministers could only regard radical criticisms as perverse. Those who proposed alternatives had to be denied lest, tinkering with the mechanics of the economic system, they drop spanners in the works and make matters worse. As a consequence of this attitude political life between the wars was largely concerned with the exclusion by the orthodox of the dissenters in the wings, and the exchange of office between Conservative and Labour members of an orthodox club.

Among the victims of this policy should be ranked Lloyd George. Described by Baldwin as 'a dynamic force . . . and a dynamic force is a very terrible thing' (104), Lloyd George had proved himself a ruthless executive during and after the war. He more than any other party leader was not afraid of power, and by 1929 he was willing to use the state's authority to force through policies which he instinctively felt to be right. According to one study Baldwin and MacDonald, for personal and party reasons, devoted much of their time to blocking off Lloyd George's possible routes back to office (95). His exclusion helped ensure the supremacy of the mediocre and the triumph of orthodoxy. A similar fate befell Mosley, another outsider unable to break through a barrier of suspicion. After his resignation his proposals came close to achieving majority support within the Labour party, but the stubborn loyalty of Labour MPs to the party leadership and its wishes ensured their final rejection (107).

Baldwin and MacDonald therefore rejected the unorthodox and disturbing, and such rejections were on the whole meekly accepted by their political followers. It is perhaps surprising that as a consequence the dissenters across the political spectrum could not unite to dethrone the establishment. One of Mosley's aims in forming the New Party in 1931 was to unite the discontented behind a common programme. He had the sympathy of Macmillan and Boothby, of Amery and Melchett and of some of his former Labour colleagues, but as well as different emphases in their respective radical plans, the dissenters were still restrained by the pull of traditional party loyalties; radical cooperation got little further than flattering reviews of each other's books and occasional appearances on the same speaking platforms.

As a final comment on the political obstacles to radical change it is noticeable that Baldwin, MacDonald and then Chamberlain continued to win the support of the electorate in the 1920s and 1930s. They were tried and not apparently found wanting. Lloyd George's campaign achieved poor results in the 1929 general election and still worse in 1935. Less regrettably, Mosley never tapped much support with the British Union of Fascists. There is no evidence to show that the Labour party would have won a general election at any time before the Second World War, in spite of its radically improved programmes and the stubborn continuation of depression (28).

Unemployment between the wars did leave some important lasting consequences. Inadequate though their responses were, governments had been forced by public opinion, political pressures and unavoidable circumstances to extend their functions. Willy-nilly, the state had increased its responsibilities. The cover of its welfare policy had been widened by extensions of unemployment insurance, especially by the principles of dependants' allowances and of continuous tax-financed assistance for the long-term unemployed. Its range of economic duties had grown with a managed currency, tariffs, sporadic help for industry and a gesture towards a regional aid policy. At all events, the government had intervened in the free market, no matter how distasteful they found the experience. Baldwin himself confessed in 1935 that 'for good or evil the days of non-interference by Governments are gone. We are passing into a new era' (110).

There were many commentators who recognised, often more clearly than ministers, the implications of these innovations. They served as precedents. In the new thinking which emerged between the wars, government was given an increasingly predominant role. For this, the unemployment problem was largely responsible. It stimulated more people to examine the social conditions of Britain and to discover what baleful effects the depression was having on workers. They disagreed in their assessments of the latter but did reveal the extent to which poverty and ill-health from various causes were still common. They concluded that existing welfare services were inadequate. Even before the Second World War therefore, proposals were being made, not just for more extensions of state services to help the unemployed, but to deal with a host of other social problems that researchers had unearthed. The need for a national nutritional policy, improved housing, better medical care, family allowances were all under discussion. The Second World War then made them parts of more extensive reconstruction plans **(59) [doc. 29]** . The origins of the postwar welfare state are to be found therefore in the discoveries and proposals which interwar unemployment not exclusively but substantially generated. The Beveridge report on Social Insurance, for example, was written by a man who had been a student of unemployment since before the First World War and who was made secretary of the Unemployment Insurance Statutory Committee on its formation in 1934 **(99)**.

Equally, the depression and tentative government reactions to it inspired radical plans for state economic management and state industrial planning. It was no longer possible for innovators to see solutions to economic problems like unemployment which did not require a major contribution by the state. Indeed by the end of the 1930s even the Treasury was more sympathetic to such notions **(69, 70)**. The Second World War effectively proved the value of such radical plans. Churchill made Keynes an adviser at the Treasury in 1940, and the techniques he recommended then governed the way the economy was managed in the crisis. It was apparent that they worked. As a result, they seemed to promise a sure way of avoiding unemployment in the future, and were integrated into plans for the postwar world. Keynesian methods of economic management were the basis of Beveridge's *Full Employment in a Free Society* (1944), the Coalition government's white paper *Employment Policy* (1944) and the proposals put by all parties to the electorate in 1945 **(59, 81)**.

The distress mass unemployment had caused between the wars left a lasting impression on popular attitudes. After 1945 ministers accepted a commitment to maintain full employment, not only because it now seemed practicable, but because it was evidently expected of them. Having tasted five years of full employment, albeit during the war, and no longer believing the problem insoluble, people were determined to avoid a return to the days of depression. The swing to Labour in the 1945 general election was partly because that party was thought more likely to honour its pledge to maintain employment levels than the Conservatives who had dominated the now despised National government **(59) [doc. 30]** . Furthermore, interwar experience probably redoubled working-class determination to achieve some measure of job security. Even though overmanning was and remains a problem in some

British industries and a restraint on economic growth, the overriding objective of many trade union leaders after the war was to oppose redundancies and fight for security of employment.

Once immediate postwar problems were overcome, the country enjoyed considerable prosperity. How far this was due to government policies is open to debate. Nevertheless unemployment in Britain remained low; not until the 1970s did numbers increase substantially. When they did it generated new alarm. In part this was because, in spite of the cushion of welfare services, unemployment remains for most workers a grim ordeal. The mental stresses felt by the unemployed today are much as they were between the wars. Work retains its social as well as its economic value to the worker. But those who protest against unemployment are also angry with a government which they feel is breaking the code of practice followed since 1945 in allowing the revival of a suppressed evil. Unemployment has again become a politically sensitive issue. To a great extent this is another legacy from the interwar depression. For many people the memory of those years remains close and bitter, and they resent the return to a high rate of unemployment.

Part Four: Documents

document 1

The image of the unemployed

Greenwood's novel presented a bleak picture of the distress caused by unemployment. This has proved a lasting image of Britain between the wars.

It got you slowly, with the slippered stealth of an unsuspected, malignant disease.

You fell into the habit of slouching, of putting your hands into your pockets and keeping them there; of glancing at people, furtively, ashamed of your secret, until you fancied that everybody eyed you with suspicion. You knew that your shabbiness betrayed you; it was apparent for all to see. You prayed for the winter evenings and the kindly darkness. Darkness, poverty's cloak. Breeches backside patched and re-patched; patches on knees, on elbows. Jesus! All bloody patches. Gor' blimey! ...

Nothing to do with time; nothing to spend; nothing to do to-morrow nor the day after; nothing to wear; can't get married. A living corpse; a unit of the spectral army of three million lost men.

Walter Greenwood, **(35)**, pp. 224–5.

document 2

A land of contrasts

Returning from a tour of the country in 1933, Priestley summed up his impressions of its varied face.

There was, first, old England, the country of the cathedrals and minsters and manor houses and inns, of Parson and Squire; guide-book and quaint highways and byways England.... Then, I decided, there is the nineteenth-century England, the industrial England of coal, iron, steel, cotton, wool, railways; of thousands of rows of little houses all alike, sham Gothic churches, square-faced chapels, Town Halls, Mechanics' Institutes, mills, foundries, warehouses . . . a cynically devastated country side, sooty dismal little towns, and still sootier grim fortress-like cities. This England makes up the larger part of the Midlands and the North and exists everywhere; but it is not being added to and has no new life poured into it. . . . The third England, I concluded, was the new post-war England, belonging far more to the age itself than to this particular island. America, I supposed, was its real birth-place. This is the England of arterial and by-pass roads, of filling stations and factories that look like exhibition buildings, of giant cinemas and dance-halls and cafes, bungalows with tiny garages, cocktail bars, Woolworths, motor-coaches, wireless, hiking, factory girls looking like actresses. . . .

J.B. Priestley, (51) pp. 397–9, 401.

document 3
Lost exports and Lancashire

The problems of the staple industries were analysed in many contemporary publications. In this account Professor Allen of the University College of Hull describes the troubles of the Lancashire cotton industry.

It is on the loss of foreign trade that attention must be concentrated, for this has been the main cause of the deep depression in the industry. . . . In the foreign markets, in spite of the development of an export trade in mixed fabrics, there has been no adequate compensation for the heavy losses sustained in the main classes of goods. . . . The chief losses had occurred in the export of cheap goods to India, China, the Balkans and the Near East; while the exports to countries taking high-priced products had suffered little. . . . Thus, Lancashire's loss has been due, first, to the opportunities given by the war to Oriental producers, and secondly to the shifting of demand in the bulk-goods trade from the type of goods which Lancashire has been accustomed to supply to cheaper goods of a different kind, in the manufacture of which Oriental producers have greater advantages.

G.C. Allen, *British Industries and Their Organization*, Longmans 1st edn, 1933, pp. 219–20, 224.

Tyneside

This is an extract from one of the many regional studies undertaken between the wars. It was made for the Bureau of Social Research for Tyneside.

It is easy now, in the light of what has happened since, to realise that the pre-War position of Tyneside was precarious. Precarious because it was so largely based upon a few great industries; precarious, also, because it depended to such an extent upon the demands of foreign countries, which might begin to supply themselves; and precarious because so much of the industry was due to the race in armaments which could not continue indefinitely.... During the whole time of the writing of this report Tyneside has been in deep depression, though latterly there has been some improvement. The outlook for coal and for shipbuilding are discussed in following chapters where it is argued that at best there can be no rapid expansion for a good many years whilst in each case contraction is possible. The outlook for the armament industry is, of course, worse still.... A restoration of the pre-War position is, therefore, almost an impossibility for Tyneside.... The necessity for broadening again the basis of Tyneside's livelihood has been forced home to everyone during the depression of trade, and there has been much discussion as to possible new industries and methods of attracting manufacturers to the area.

H.A. Mess, *Industrial Tyneside*, Benn 1928, pp. 41–3, 48.

The regional impact

National averages of unemployment disguise contrasting regional economic fortunes.

Once again the south and midlands claimed the greater part of the expansion of working population.... The effect of this unequal expansion is more readily seen by taking a long-term view. Since 1923 the 'south' group has grown between three and four times as fast as the 'north' group, with the result that the proportion of the country's workers aged 16–64 who are in the south has risen during this period from 45.7 per cent to 51 per cent. . . . Contrary to a widespread impression, the greater expansion of the south is not primarily caused by the wholesale migration of workers from less prosperous areas in search of employment: the case is rather that new enterprise has tended to look favourably upon the south when determining its location and a higher proportion of the local population has been attracted into insurable employment.

The greater prosperity of the south is reflected also in the relative incidence of unemployment. In December the rate of unemployment among insured persons aged 16–64 in the country as a whole was a little below 12 per cent. On the other hand, all the northern groups were less fortunate than the national average. . . . Broadly speaking, the incidence of unemployment was twice as severe in the north, excepting the north eastern division and three times as severe in Wales as in the south.

Ministry of Labour, *Report for the Year 1937*, Cmd, 5717, 1938, pp.4–5.

document 6

Who were the unemployed?

One of the best studies of the unemployed was carried out by the Pilgrim Trust. Here they record which groups of workers suffered most from long-term unemployment.

TABLE V	
Men Only	How many per 1000 workers were unemployed for a year or more in the summer of 1936?
1 Coal miners	123
2 Ship-builders and repairers	95
3 Cotton workers	67
4 Seamen	59
5 Pig-iron and Iron and Steel workers	57
6 Pottery and Earthenware workers	54
7 Workers in Textile Bleaching, Dyeing, etc.	37
8 Waiters and other workers in Hotels, Public houses and Restaurants	33
9 Gas, Water and Electricity workers	33
10 Boot and Shoe workers	31
11 General Engineering	31
12 Dock and Harbour workers	27
13 Workers in Distributive Trades	27
14 Workers in Bread, Biscuits, Cakes, etc.	26
15 Workers in Tailoring firms	25
16 Builders and Building Labourers	24
17 Furniture workers	21
18 Printers, Bookbinders	14
19 Workers in Motor Vehicles, Cycles, etc.	10
All Workers	41

The facts, for June 1936, were as shown in Table V. The major industries which contribute most heavily to the queues of unemployed men can be clearly seen from this table, and the close connexion between long unemployment and industrial decline is obvious. Indeed . . . at least 40% of the long unemployment throughout the country is concentrated in the four basic and (in the post-War period) structurally declining industries, coal-mining, ship-building, iron and steel, textile manufacture.

The Pilgrim Trust, (50), pp. 17–18.

document 7

The poverty of the unemployed

Prominent among the vehement critics of government policy in the 1930s was Wal Hannington, leader of the National Unemployed Workers Movement.

Take a look at a funeral procession in South Wales these days. The custom is for the relations and friends to walk behind the hearse to the cemetery, and the miners, who in times of good trade always had a preference for smart blue serge suits, would turn out in their best apparel and bowler hats, and present an exceedingly respectable appearance. But not so to-day. A funeral procession in the Rhondda Valley bears the mark of extreme poverty. The few serge suits which are seen can be marked out by their cut as pre-war or immediate post-war, because for years no new clothes have been bought.

Wal Hannington, (37), p. 72.

document 8

Robbing the 'dirt-train'

The techniques whereby the unemployed tried to supplement their dole money were many. Orwell came upon this method in Wigan in February 1936.

This afternoon with Paddy Grady to see the unemployed miners robbing the 'dirt-train', or, as they call it, 'scrambling for the coal'. A most astonishing sight. We went by the usual frightful routes along the colliery railway line to Fir Tree sidings. . . . When we got there we found not less than 100 men, a few boys, waiting. . . . Presently the train hove in sight, coming round the bend at about 20 m.p.h. 50 or 70 men rushed for it, seized hold of the bumpers etc. and hoisted themselves on to the trucks. . . . The engine ran the trucks up on to the dirt-heap, uncoupled them and came back for the remaining trucks. There was the same wild rush and the second train was boarded in the same manner. . . . As soon as the trucks had been uncoupled the men on top began shovelling the stuff out to their women and other supporters below, who rapidly sorted out the dirt and put all the coal (a considerable amount but all small, in lumps about the size of eggs) into their sacks. . . .

Some of this coal that is stolen is said to be on sale in the town at
1s 6d. a bag.

George Orwell, **(47)**, pp. 181–3.

document 9

Diets

*Rowntree, like other investigators, compared the diet of families living
in poverty with the dietetic needs defined by nutrition experts.*

This family consists of a man aged 41, his wife aged 36 and four children
aged 14, 6, 4 and 20 months. The man has been out of work throughout
the year and the sole source of income of the family is his unemployment benefit of 36s. a week, with an occasional odd shilling earned
by his wife. . . .

MENU OF MEALS PROVIDED

	Breakfast	*Dinner*	*Tea*	*Supper*
FRIDAY	Bread and dripping, tea	Fish cod (1) and potatoes, bread and butter and tea	Bread and butter, tomatoes, jam, tea	None
SATUR-DAY	Bacon (2), bread and dripping, tea	Minced meat (3) and potatoes, bread and butter, tea	Bread and butter, potted meat tea	Cocoa
SUNDAY	Bacon, bread and dripping, tea	Roast meat (4) kidney beans, potatoes, Yorkshire pudding	Bread and butter, stewed plums and jelly, shortcakes, tea	Cocoa
MON-DAY	Bread and dripping, tea	Cold meat and potatoes, bread and butter, tea	Bread and butter, shortcakes, jam, tea	Cocoa
TUES-DAY	Bread and dripping, tea	Meat hash, tea	Bread and butter, shortcakes, tea	Cocoa
WEDNES-DAY	Bread and dripping, tea	Liver (5) and onions, potatoes, tea	Bread and butter, and beetroot, tea	Cocoa

THURS-DAY	Bread and dripping, tea	Sausages (6) and potatoes, tea	Bread and butter, jam, tea	Cocoa

(1) 2 lbs. fish
(2) ½ lb. bacon gives meals for two mornings
(3) ½ lb. minced beef
(4) 2 lbs. beef is spread over three days
(5) ½ lb. liver
(6) ½ lb. beef sausages
Only three have supper

COMMENTS ON THE DIETARY

	s.	d.
The average weekly expenditure on food is	16	10
To feed this family adequately on the standard diet would cost	24	3½

The diet shows a deficiency in first-class protein and calories of 51.2 per cent and 27.7 per cent respectively. There is a serious deficiency in mineral salts and of vitamins A and B_1.

B.S. Rowntree, (52), pp. 188–9.

document 10

Health

The effect of unemployment on health was vigorously debated. Government investigators were on the whole blandly reassuring.

The primary object of our visit . . . was to ascertain whether as a result of unemployment in the coalfield the physical condition in any section of the population was such as to call for special action. . . . The first question to which it was obvious that we ought to direct our attention was that of any variation to be observed in the rates of mortality in South Wales and Monmouth indicating new conditions exceptionally injurious to health. No such indications are forthcoming from the general death rates. Further, there has been no unusual mortality from epidemic diseases. . . . On the criterion of infant mortality, . . . there are no figures showing that the health of this region is suffering or need give rise to anxiety. . . . There has been no obvious growth in the prevalence of [tuberculosis] . . . . As regards what are specially termed 'deficiency diseases', there was no evidence of the existence of scurvy, and the only form belonging to this category which appeared to have shown signs of increase was rickets. . . . The increase nowhere affects a large proportion of the child population. . . . Although apart from rickets we could find nothing to indicate an increase in any particular disease, and although there is no evidence of obvious and widespread deterioration of physique, there could be no question that in some areas women, especially the mothers of young children, suffer to an unusual extent from languor and anaemia. We were also not infrequently told that there is a loss of tone and persistence of debility after illness in the older men, and that men long unemployed who have not been actually ill find resumption of work difficult as a mere physical effort.

Ministry of Health, (42), pp. 3–6.

document 11

Mental health

It was widely accepted that mental strain was a common consequence of unemployment. Here the Pilgrim Trust record the view of a medical officer.

His opinion was that the principal effects of prolonged unemployment on the health of the unemployed men themselves were a subtle undermining of the constitution through lack of physical exertion, the absence of physical stimuli, insufficiently varied diet, and worry; and the emergence of abnormal psychological conditions characterized by disabling fears, anxieties, and sympathetic physical conditions, functional disorders and the like. He gave a number of striking examples of local men who had been apparently normal when in work, but who had 'gone to pieces' after being unemployed for several years. The following cases are a few of the many which were quoted:

(i) Man, single, aged 40. In normal health until unemployed. After four years' unemployment complained of choking and pains in the head, but specialist reported no lesion. . . . Only psychological explanation adequate.

(ii) Man, married (with family), aged 50. In normal health until unemployed. Developed constant aches and pains in head and became a chronic neurasthenic.

(iii) Man, single, aged 22. Normal health until unemployed. Began to suffer from 'vague fears' after period of unemployment. Was admitted to hospital. Neurosis diagnosed.

Pilgrim Trust, **(50)**, p. 137.

document 12

Starvation

Hutt admits that this story, taken from the Daily Worker *of 30 January 1933, is an extreme case, but he cites it as evidence of the devastating poverty caused by unemployment and government policy.*

How an unemployed man's wife literally starved herself to death for her children was told at an inquest on Mrs Minnie Annie Weaving, aged 37, of Elmscott-Road, Downham, S.E. George Henry Weaving, the husband, said his wife had not seen a doctor since July, when she had twins. They had seven children living. On Monday she complained of pain, but refused to see a doctor. On Wednesday she said she would get up to bath the twins, and he went to get a doctor. On his return he found his wife dead and the children crying around her. Major Whitehouse (the coroner): 'Did she have enough to eat?' — 'That is the trouble with us all. I am out of work.' Mr Weaving said he was drawing the dole, 35s.3d. a week, and was getting 5s. from the Relieving Officer. His little girl was earning 8s. a week. He had been taken to court for arrears of rent, and had to pay two weeks in one. He was now paying three weeks in two. Major Whitehouse: 'I should call it starving to have to feed nine people on £2.8s. a week and pay the rent.' Dr Arthur Davies, pathologist, of Harley-Street, W., said Mrs Weaving's body was much wasted. Death was due to pneumonia. He added: 'I have no doubt that had she had sufficient food this attack would not have proved fatal. It appears that she deliberately stinted herself and gave such food as came into the house to the children, and so sacrificed her life.'

Allen Hutt, **(38)**, p. 153.

document 13

Escape

An American investigator asked unemployed men in Greenwich in 1931–2 how they filled their days without work.

'What attracts you to the cinema?' . . . 'The pictures help you live in another world for a little while. I almost feel I'm in the picture.' . . . 'Pictures are my first choice, because they make you think for a little while that life is all right.' 'The pictures remind you that things go right for some folks, and it really makes you feel that things will go all right for you, too, because you put yourself in the place of the actors.' . . .

Numerous replies of this nature leave little doubt that the continuous appeal of the movie is that it satisfies the desire for new experience and a glimpse of other worlds and at times an escape from the present environment. This satisfaction is doubly important to the man whose world is severely limited because of the smallness of income or the total absence of earned income because of unemployment. At work and at home his activity and thought must run in rather straight grooves. Very often these grooves pass through some very unpleasant territory. But at the cinema, all of these limitations drop away and for three hours he rides the plains of Arizona, tastes the night life of Paris or New York, makes a safe excursion into the underworld, sails the seven seas or penetrates the African jungle. Famous comedians make him laugh and forget his difficulties and discouragements.

It does not surprise me that the cinemas noticed very little falling off of trade in Greenwich or in other communities more subject to unemployment during the severest seasons of that scourge.

E.W. Bakke, (31) pp. 181–3.

document 14
Family life

In a series of articles originally published in The Listener *in 1933, workers described the effects of unemployment upon them. Here the pessimistic view of the consequences for family life is illustrated by the misfortune of a skilled engineer, married for twenty years.*

In the meantime my wife had decided to try and earn a little money so that we might continue to retain our home. She obtained a job as house to house saleswoman, and was able to earn a few shillings to supplement our dole income. It was from this time that the feeling of strain which was beginning to appear in our home life became more marked. I felt a burden on her. . . . Life became more and more strained. There were constant bickerings over money matters usually culminating in threats to leave from both of us. The final blow came when the Means Test was put into operation. I realised that if I told the Exchange that my wife was earning a little they might reduce my benefit. If that happened home life would become impossible. When, therefore, I was sent a form on which to give details of our total income I neglected to fill it up. For this I was suspended benefit for six weeks. This was the last straw. Quarrels broke out anew and bitter things were said. Eventually, after the most heartbreaking period of my lfe, both my wife and my son, who had just commenced to earn a few shillings, told me to get out, as I was living on them and taking the food they needed.

H.L. Beales and R.S. Lambert, (32), pp. 73—4.

document 15
Crime

From the same source we have the story of a young man who attributes his turning to crime as a consequence of unemployment.

Until I reached the age of twenty one . . . I was an apprenticed electrician. . . . This life was rudely smashed when my firm refused to pay me a man's wage on my reaching twenty-one. . . . I gave in my notice and left the firm. . . . Eighteen months unemployment found me almost friendless. . . . I spent most of my time wandering around the streets or going to the market place to listen to the cheap-jacks selling their wares. I went so often I became friendly with some of them. . . . On one of these occasions, after my remarking on the extraordinary low price at which he was able to sell his goods, he told me that most of his stuff was stolen. . . . Within a few months I had taken part in some of their activities. There was no question of older men leading a young man astray. I found my life at that time impossible. I had nothing to look forward to. I saw myself getting lower and lower, and I took the only chance that was open to me to live. . . . Some of the people I meet have been criminal almost from birth, but I estimate that 50 per cent have drifted into burglary through bad economic conditions. . . . Strange though it seems I feel I am *somebody*, and I certainly never felt that during my two years of honest idleness.

H.L. Beales and R.S. Lambert, (32), pp. 248—54.

document 16

Political apathy

The hunger marches and violent demonstrations which sporadically impressed the general public and disturbed the government are well-known. But there is evidence to show that lethargy and political apathy were more widespread responses to unemployment. An enquiry conducted for the Carnegie U.K. Trust in Glasgow, Cardiff and Liverpool revealed these characteristics among many young men in 1936–9.

Most of the men were 21 years of age and over and, therefore, their political right to full democratic citizenship was established. . . . Out of a total of 1490 young unemployed men for whom information was available, only 20 . . . were attached in membership to one or other of the political organisations. . . . At least 10 per cent of the young men did not even know the names of the various political parties. . . . The overwhelming majority of the men had no political convictions whatsoever. When asked why, they invariably replied, 'What does it matter?' . . . It has, perhaps, been assumed too readily by some that, because men are unemployed, their natural state of want and discontent must express itself in some revolutionary attitude. It cannot be reiterated too often that unemployment is not an active state; its keynote is boredom — a continuous sense of boredom. This boredom was invariably accompanied by a disbelief which gave rise to cynicism. . . . These young men (products of continuous unemploy[ment] or privileged to enjoy only casual employment), were not likely to believe that their own active participation in affairs would permanently affect an order of things that had already, in the most impressionable years of their lives, shown itself to be so powerful and so devastating. . . . It was brought home, once again, how years of idleness bring with them acquiescence.

Carnegie U.K. Trust, (33), pp. 78–9.

document 17

Voluntary services

In most parts of the country, even outside the major depressed areas, some facilities were provided for the unemployed by local councils and voluntary organisations.

The Unemployed Welfare Committee met in the Council Chamber on

Tuesday morning. . . . The Social Centre continued to be a great boon to the men, and new bagatelle tables had been secured through Councillor R.W. Thompson. A tennis table was also being provided. . . . Another football match had been arranged, namely the Social Club v Llandudno Wednesday. . . . The question of the physical culture class came into the reports of both the Social and Educational Committees, the Rev. H. Harris Hughes agreeing with Mr Tipton that the response for volunteers for the class was very disappointing. . . . During the discussion, it was stated that one reason the class had not succeeded was that the heavy boots worn by the men were not suitable, and it was decided that the officials should take steps to obtain a few pairs of gymnastic shoes for the men joining a class. . . . Reporting on the industrial side of the work, Mr Thomas Jones specially commented on the diligence of the members of the mat-making class, and again invited orders. . . . The position with regard to finding allotments for the 25 new applications received this year was considered. . . . Another matter arising out of the report of the Educational Committee, was that of arranging a month's course for three men at Coleg Harlech. . . . The unemployed figures presented to the Committee showed that the total number (male and female) was 732.

Llandudno Advertiser 3 Feb. 1934.

document 18

The Labour Government

The orthodoxy of the Labour government in 1924 contrasts with the radicalism of some of the party's earlier proposals.

We shall concentrate, not first of all on the relief of unemployment, but on the restoration of trade. We are not going to diminish industrial capital in order to provide relief. . . . I wish to make it perfectly clear that the Government have no intention of drawing off from the normal channels of trade large sums for extemporised measures which can only be palliatives. That is the old, sound, Socialist doctrine, and the necessity of expenditure for subsidising schemes in direct relief of unemployment will be judged in relation to the greater necessity for maintaining undisturbed the ordinary financial facilities and resources of trade and industry. (Hon. Members: 'Hear, hear!')

The Prime Minister, Ramsay MacDonald, 12 Feb. 1924, *Hansard*, House of Commons, vol. 169, cols 759–60.

document 19

Reducing government expenditure

The possibility of stimulating economic recovery by government spending was largely ruled out between the wars by orthodox theory. The Treasury regularly urged government departments to restrict their expenditure.

It is, therefore, clear that very drastic steps must be taken to reduce expenditure by 1922–3.

The only alternatives to reduction of expenditure are:

(a) Fresh borrowing which, in addition to increasing the charge for interest, would mean renewed inflation, with its attendant evils, including the depression of the £ sterling at home and abroad

(b) Increased taxation. It is certain that any increase in taxation would seriously hamper the recovery of British industry and commerce and thus ultimately intensify the difficulty of the position and would on that account be most vehemently opposed by the House of Commons and by public opinion in the country; indeed what is required in order to maintain and stimulate industry and commerce – and secure full and regular employment in the country – is a reduction of taxation and of the burden of the state's indebtedness as rapidly as possible, a process which can only be achieved by a continuous reduction of expenditure throughout the next few years.

Treasury circular to Government Departments, 13 May 1921, CAB 24/123/CP 2919.

document 20

Return to the gold standard

Before deciding to put Britain back on gold, Winston Churchill demanded a justification for the policy from his senior Treasury advisers.

The most serious argument against the return to the gold standard is the feared effect on trade and employment. No one would advocate such a return if he believed that in the long run the effect on trade would be adverse.

In fact everyone upholds the gold standard, because they believe it to be proved by experience to be best for trade....

No one believes th .t unemployment can be cured by the dole, and palliatives like road digging. Every party – not least Labour – has preached that unemployment can only be dealt with by radical measures directed to the economic restoration of trade, whether with Europe or with the Dominions. What could be worse for trade than for us to have a different standard of value to South Africa and Australia . . . or to Germany and the United States – fluctuating while they are stable *inter se*? On a long view – and it is only such views that can produce fundamental cures – the gold standard is in direct succession to the main steps towards economic reconstruction (Brussels Resolutions: Austrian and Hungarian Loans: Dawes Scheme) and is likely to do more for British trade than all the efforts of the Unemployment [*Grants*] Committee.

Memo by Sir Otto Niemeyer, 2 Feb. 1925, quoted in D.E. Moggridge, *British Monetary Policy 1924–1931*, Cambridge University Press 1972, pp. 68–9.

document 21

The imperial vision

Amery was the leading spokesman of the imperial visionary school between the wars. His disappointment at the rushed election of 1923 and the Conservative defeat was compounded afterwards by the party's decision to abandon the tariff protection policy.

That decision does not, however, alter the permanent facts of the situation. Unemployment is still there. . . . Sooner or later the country will have to face the problem in earnest. When it does it will realise that there can be no security for the employment of our industries and the wages of our working population under the monstrously one-sided Free Imports now in force.

Apart from immediate security to our existing industries the one assured hope of future growth and of an improvement in the national standard of well-being lies in the development of the resources of the British Empire by mutual co-operation. That co-operation may take many forms. But Imperial Preference is essential to the success of all of them. The Free Trade obsession bars the way to any effective extension of Empire Preference and Empire Co-operation.

Leo Amery to Stanley Baldwin, 11 Feb. 1924, Amery Papers Box G.82

document 22
We can conquer unemployment

In their defence of the Liberal plans, Keynes and Henderson attacked a number of basic assumptions of orthodox thinking.

The objection, which is raised more frequently, perhaps, than any other, is that money raised by the State for financing productive schemes must diminish *pro tanto* the supply of capital available for ordinary industry. If this is true, a policy of national development will not really increase employment. It will merely substitute employment on State schemes for ordinary employment. Either that, or (so the argument often runs) it must mean inflation. . . .

In relation to the actual facts of to-day, this argument is, we believe, quite without foundation.

In the first place, there is nothing in the argument which limits its applicability to State-promoted undertakings. If it is valid at all, it must apply equally to a new works started by Morris, or Courtaulds, to any new business enterprise entailing capital expenditure. . . . We should have to conclude that these enterprising business-men were merely diverting capital from other uses, and that no real gain to employment could result. Indeed we should be driven to a still more remarkable conclusion. We should have to conclude that it was virtually out of the question to absorb our unemployed workpeople by any means whatsoever (other than the unthinkable inflation), and that the obstacle which barred the path was no other than an insufficiency of capital. This, if you please, in Great Britain, who has surplus savings which she is accustomed to lend abroad on the scale of more than a hundred millions a year.

J.M. Keynes and H.D. Henderson, (87), pp. 34–5.

document 23
Under-consumption

John Hobson had been criticising orthodox economic theory since the 1890s. In this pamphlet, he joined other members of the Independent Labour Party to explain why an increase in mass purchasing power was needed if depression was to be prevented.

All of us realise that the low purchasing power of so many millions of wage earners is among the most potent causes of the widespread unemployment which has cursed our country during the last six years. Indeed, the argument that any reduction of wages must limit the home market and aggravate unemployment, is continually used by every body of workers in combating wage cuts. . . .

Low wages mean a limitation of the home market. The benefits of mass production cannot be realised to the full, because the power of the masses to consume fails to keep pace with the power of the machines to produce. . . . We produce less wealth than our technical resources would enable us to create, because the mass of the wage-earners lack 'effective demand'. The owning class has misused the advantage of its position. Too much, proportionately, of the product of industry, has been accumulated and applied to the creation of fresh instruments of production: too little, proportionately, has gone in wages to make a market for the product of these new machines. . . . The practical conclusion from this familiar analysis of the vices of the industrial system, as we know it in this country, is that by one expedient or another we must aim at a general and simultaneous increase in the purchasing power of the masses.

H.N. Brailsford, *et al*, (83), pp. 2, 8.

document 24

Rationalisation

Jarrow's principal industry was destroyed as part of a rationalisation programme for the shipbuilding industry. The plight of the town was ably publicised by the local MP, Ellen Wilkinson, and the Jarrow Hunger March of 1936.

On February 28, 1930, the first public statement was made regarding National Shipbuilders' Security, Ltd. Its purpose was defined as being to assist the shipbuilding industry by the purchase of redundant or obsolete yards. To ensure that the productive capacity of the industry was definitely reduced the shipbuilding equipment was to be scrapped and the site of the yard was to be restricted against further use for shipbuilding. . . .

In the early summer of 1934 it was announced that Palmer's had been sold to N.S.S. The death warrant of Palmer's was signed. The reason for Jarrow's existence had vanished overnight.

Why was Palmer's Yard sold? It certainly was not an obsolete yard.

One of the biggest firms in the industry and one which had invariably secured a fair share on competitive tenders cannot be classed as obsolete. It had one of the finest sites in the country. . . . Financial weakness, and not technical inefficiency, decided the fate of the company. The rationalization of the shipbuilding industry has been carried through in that way — with an eye on the balance sheet rather than on the efficiency of the particular companies. . . .

Sold by National Shipbuilding Security [*sic*] to a demolition firm, work was commenced to clear the site. Oxy-acetylene burners made short work of steel girders. Cranes crashed to the ground, the machine shops were emptied, the blast furnaces and their numerous chimneys were demolished. The familiar overhead cranes vanished. For forty years, shipbuilding is exiled from Jarrow.

Ellen Wilkinson (**58**), pp. 149, 161—3.

document 25

Industrial transference

The hardening of official attitudes against the relief of unemployment by public works can be seen in the Industrial Transference Board's opposition to the work of the Unemployment Grants Committee.

As an essential condition for the growth of the will to move, nothing should be done which might tend to anchor men to their home district by holding out an illusory prospect of employment. We therefore reject as unsound policy relief works in the depressed areas. Such schemes are temporary; at the end the situation is much as before, and the financial resources either of the Exchequer or of the Local Authorities have been drained to no permanent purpose. Grants of assistance such as those made by the Unemployment Grants Committee, which help to finance works carried out by the Local Authority in depressed areas, for the temporary employment of men in those areas, are a negation of the policy which ought in our opinion to be pursued.

Industrial Transference Board, *Report*, Cmd 3156, 1928, p. 18.

document 26

The Special Areas Acts

In his third report in November 1936 the Commissioner for England

and Wales reviewed progress to date and went on to comment on the inadequacy of the commission's existing power.

There is evidence that the work done and the measures initiated are proving helpful to the Areas and that their benefits will in many cases be increasingly felt. Nevertheless, it has to be admitted that no appreciable reduction of the number of those unemployed has been effected. This, however, was not to be looked for seeing that the Special Areas Act makes no direct provision for this purpose. Such increased employment as is likely to result from the operation of the many schemes initiated will prove altogether insufficient, in the absence of a spontaneous growth of new industries and expansion of existing industries, to offset the release of labour brought about by increased mechanisation and rationalisation. . . .

The all-important question that arises from a study of the results obtained from its administration is whether the time is not now ripe for a second experiment which, whilst continuing work already embarked upon, would make an attempt to deal more directly with the problem of unemployment. . . . My recommendation is that by means of State-provided inducements a determined attempt should be made to attract industrialists to the Special Areas.

Third Report of the Commissioner for the Special Areas (England and Wales), Cmd 5303, 1936, pp. 3–4, 10.

document 27

Unemployment insurance

The Unemployment Act of 1934 was the twenty-first Act to deal with unemployment insurance since 1920, an indication of the difficulty administrations experienced in coping with the depression.

I regard this as one of the most comprehensive and constructive pieces of social legislation which have been introduced into this House for many generations. . . .

The Bill is based on the fundamental principle . . . that there should be, on the one hand, a contributory insurance scheme covering as much of the field as possible, and that outside insurance the State should assume a general responsibility for the relief of the able-bodied industrial unemployed. . . . First of all, let me put to the House the three broad principles on which Part 1 – insurance – is based. . . .

1. That the scheme should be financed by contributions from the workers, employers and the state;
2. That benefit should be dependent upon contributions;
3. That the scheme should be maintained on a solvent and seif-supporting basis. . . .

I will now deal . . . with Part II of the Bill, and I will attempt . . . to explain the three principles which underlie it . . . first, that assistance should be proportionate to need; secondly, that a worker who has been long unemployed may require assistance other than, and in addition to, cash payments, and, thirdly, that the State should accept general responsibility for all the industrial able-bodied unemployed outside insurance.

The Minister of Labour, Sir Henry Betterton, 30 Nov. 1933, *Hansard*, vol. 283, cols 1073, 1077–8, 1087.

document 28

The middle way

Macmillan analysed the growing intimacy between the state and industry and the nature of large modern corporations. He concluded that full employment and future prosperity would inevitably require state planning and fiscal and monetary management.

The facts I have been able to bring together . . . show that it is impossible to regard the real issue of today as being that of a struggle between the theories of free competition and planned production – between *laissez-faire* and State intervention. While political parties – like Tweedledum and Tweedledee – have been conducting the theoretical argument, the two systems have in practice merged. Competition and planned production, State enterprise and private enterprise, exist side by side. . . . I believe it to be politically wise and economically urgent for us now to devise a comprehensive system of national planning into which the operations of all the separate schemes of partial planning, whether under National, Public Utility, Municipal or Private ownership and control, should be made to fit as integral parts of a coherent whole.

Harold Macmillan **(90)**, pp. 173–4, 186–7.

document 29
'A Plan for Britain'

Interwar ideas on state planning and management formed the basis of most wartime reconstruction proposals. Picture Post *published 'A Plan for Britain' early in 1941, including an article by Thomas Balogh, now Lord Balogh, on the need to provide 'The first necessity in the New Britain: work for all'.*

Why then were we faced in a comparatively short space of time after 1918 by a vast unemployment problem? The fact is that in 1918 the sufferings of four years produced an urgent desire to be rid of everything that war meant, and led to a demand for an instant abolition of all State controls, however well they had functioned. ...

It was every man for himself, whether he wanted to find a job, or whether he wanted to invest money in the work of reconstruction which caused the postwar boom. Nobody could bother to plan the supply of labour for this work. Nobody could bother to plan the work itself on a national scale. ... And afterwards, when the frenzy of speculation had exhausted itself, came the crash. ...

Now, we must learn the lesson of what happened last time and decide firmly that it shall not happen again. ... Reconstruction must be planned exactly as war production ought to be planned.

Picture Post, 4 Jan. 1941, pp. 10–12.

document 30
Never again

After the Second World War both leading political parties committed themselves to the maintenance of full employment.

Labour ... declares that full employment is the corner-stone of the new society.

The Labour Government has ensured full employment and fair shares of the necessities of life. What a contrast with pre-war days! In those days millions of unwanted men eked out their lives in need of the very things they themselves could have made in the factories that were standing idle.

Even when at work each man often feared that the next pay-day would be the last. The wife feared that the housekeeping money would suddenly vanish. Often it did. Her husband was handed his cards, he drew the dole, then she had to make do with a fraction of her previous money — and despite all her sacrifices the children suffered. . . .

Whatever our Party, all of us old enough to remember are in our hearts ashamed of those years. They were unhappy years for our country and our people. They must never come again.

Labour Party manifesto, *Let Us Win Through Together*, 1950, repr. in F.W.S. Craig, *British General Election Manifestos 1918–1966*, Political Reference Publications, 1970, p. 127.

Bibliography

GENERAL POLITICAL, SOCIAL AND ECONOMIC HISTORY

1   Abrams, M., *The Condition of the British People 1911–1945*, Gollancz, 1946.

2   Aldcroft, D.H. *The Inter-War Economy: Britain 1919–39*, Batsford, 1970.

3   Alford, B.W.E. *Depression and Recovery? British Economic Growth 1918–1939*, Macmillan, 1972.

4   Ashworth W. *An Economic History of England 1870–1939*, Methuen, 1960.

5   Bagwell, P.S. and Mingay, G.E. *Britain and America: a study of economic change 1850–1939*, Routledge & Kegan Paul, 1970.

6   Deane, P. and Cole, W.A. *British Economic Growth 1688–1959*, Cambridge University Press, 2nd edn, 1967.

7   Glynn, S. and Oxborrow, J. *Interwar Britain: a social and economic history*, Allen & Unwin, 1976.

8   Halsey, A.H., ed. *Trends in British Society since 1900*, Macmillan, 1972.

9   Mathias, P. *The First Industrial Nation*, Methuen, 1969.

10 Mitchell, B.R. and Deane, P. *Abstract of British Historical Statistics*, Cambridge University Press, 1971.

11 Mowat, C.L. *Britain Between the Wars 1918–1940*, Methuen, 1955.

12 Pollard, S. *The Development of the British Economy 1914–1967*, Arnold, 2nd edn, 1969.

13 Richardson, H.W. *Economic Recovery in Britain 1932–9*, Weidenfeld & Nicolson, 1967.

14 Sayers, R.S. *Economic Change in England 1880–1939*, Oxford University Press, 1967.

15 Stevenson, J. *Social Conditions in Britain between the Wars*, Penguin, 1977.

16 Taylor, A.J.P. *English History 1914–1945*, Oxford University Press, 1965.

THE DEPRESSION AND ITS SOCIAL CONSEQUENCES

17 Beveridge, W.H. *Full Employment in a Free Society*, Allen & Unwin, 1944.

18 Booth, A.E. and Glynn, S. 'Unemployment in the interwar period: a multiple problem', *Journal of Contemporary History*, x, 1975.

19 Department of Employment and Productivity *British Labour Statistics Historical Abstract 1886–1968*, HMSO, 1971.

20 Elliott, B.J. 'The social and economic effects of unemployment in the coal and steel industries of Sheffield between 1925 and 1935', unpublished thesis, University of Sheffield MA, 1969.

21 Garraty, J.A. 'Unemployment during the Great Depression', *Labor History*, xvii, 1976.

22 Hayburn, R.H.C. 'The responses to unemployment in the 1930s with particular reference to south-east Lancashire', unpublished thesis, University of Hull PhD, 1970.

23 Hayburn, R.H.C. 'The Voluntary Occupational Centre Movement 1932–39,' *Journal of Contemporary History*, vi, 1971.

24 Hayburn, R.H.C. 'The police and the hunger marchers', *International Review of Social History*, xvii, 1972.

25 Mannheim, H. *Social Aspects of Crime in England between the Wars*, Allen & Unwin, 1940.

26 Pope, R. 'The unemployment problem in North East Lancashire 1920–1938', unpublished thesis, University of Lancaster M Litt, 1974.

27 Runciman, W.G. *Relative Deprivation and Social Justice*, Routledge & Kegan Paul, 1966.

28 Stevenson, J. and Cook, C. *The Slump: society and politics during the Depression*, Cape, 1977.

29 Turnbull, M. 'Attitude of government and administration towards the hunger marches of the 1920s and 1930s', *Journal of Social Policy*, ii, 1973.

Primary sources

30 Astor, J.J. *et al. The Third Winter of Unemployment*, P.S. King, 1922.

31 Bakke, E.W. *The Unemployed Man*, Nisbet, 1933.

32 Beales, H.L. and Lambert, R.S., eds., *Memoirs of the Unemployed*, Gollancz, 1934.

33 Carnegie U.K. Trust *Disinherited Youth*, Constable, 1943.

34 Cole, G.D.H. and Cole, M.I. *The Condition of Britain*, Gollancz, 1937.

35 Greenwood, W. *Love on the Dole*, Cape, 1933; repr. Penguin, 1969.

36 Hannington, W. *Unemployed Struggles 1919–1936*, Lawrence & Wishart, 1936; repr. 1977.

37 Hannington, W. *The Problem of the Distressed Areas*, Left Book Club, Gollancz, 1937.

38 Hutt, A. *The Condition of the Working Class in Britain*, Martin Lawrence, 1933.

39 Jahoda, M. *et al., Marienthal: the Sociography of an unemployed community*, 1933, repr. Tavistock, 1972.

40 Jennings, H. *Brynmawr, a study of a Distressed Area*, Allenson, 1934.

41 M'Gonigle, G.C.M. and Kirby, J. *Poverty and Public Health*, Gollancz, 1936.

42 Ministry of Health *Investigation in the Coalfields of South Wales*, Cmd 3272, 1929.

43 Ministry of Health *Effects of Existing Economic Circumstances on the Health of the Community in Durham*, Cmd 4886, 1935.

44 Ministry of Health *Reports on Maternal Mortality*, Cmd, 5422 and 5423, 1937.

45 Ministry of Labour *Reports of Investigations into the Industirāl Conditions in Certain Depressed Areas*, Cmd 4728, 1934.

46 Orwell, G. *The Road to Wigan Pier*, Left Book Club, Gollancz, 1937. repr. Penguin, 1962.

47 Orwell, G. 'The Road to Wigan Pier Diary' in *Collected Essays, Journalism and Letters*, vol. 1, Secker & Warburg, 1968.

48 Owen, A.D.K. *A Report on Unemployment in Sheffield*, Sheffield Social Survey Committee, 1932.

49 Owen, A.D.K. 'The social consequences of industrial transference', *Sociological Review*, xxix, 1937.

50 Pilgrim Trust, *Men Without Work*, Cambridge University Press, 1938.

51 Priestley, J.B. *English Journey*, Heinemann/Gollancz 1934; repr. Penguin, 1977.

52 Rowntree, B.S. *Poverty and Progress*, Longmans Green 1941.

53 *Royal Commission on the Distribution of the Industrial Population* (Barlow Report), Cmd 6153, 1940.

54 Ruck, S.K. 'The increase of crime in England', *Political Quarterly*, iii, 1932.

55 Save the Children Fund, *Unemployment and the Child*, Longmans Green, 1933.

56 Titmuss, R.M. *Poverty and Population*, Macmillan, 1938.

57 Tout, H. *The Standard of Living in Bristol*, Arrowsmith, 1938.

58 Wilkinson, E. *The Town that was Murdered*, Left Book Club, Gollancz, 1939.

ECONOMIC AND SOCIAL POLICY

59 Addison, P. *The Road to 1945*, Cape, 1975.

60 Bruce, M. *The Coming of the Welfare State,* Batsford, 4th edn, 1968.

61 Cole, G.D.H. *A History of the Labour Party from 1914*, Routledge & Kegan Paul, 1948.

62 Constantine, S. 'The formulation of British policy on colonial development 1914–1929', unpublished thesis, University of Oxford D Phil, 1974.

63 Drummond, I.M. *British Economic Policy and the Empire 1919–1939*, Allen & Unwin, 1972.

64 Drummond, I.M. *Imperial Economic Policy 1917–1939*, Allen & Unwin, 1974.

65 Fraser, D. *The Evolution of the British Welfare State*, Macmillan, 1973.

66 Garside, W.R. 'Juvenile unemployment and public policy', *Economic History Review*, xxx, 1977.

67 Gilbert, B.B. *British Social Policy 1914–1939*, Batsford, 1970.

68 Hancock, K.J. 'The reduction of unemployment as a problem of public policy, 1920–1929', *Economic History Review*, xv, 1962; repr. in (77).

69 Howson, S. *Domestic Monetary Management in Britain 1919–38*, Cambridge University Press, 1975.

70 Howson, S. and Winch, D. *The Economic Advisory Council 1930–9*, Cambridge University Press, 1977.

71 Lyman, R.W. *The First Labour Government*, Chapman & Hall, 1957.

72 MacKay, D.I. *et al.* 'The discussion of public works programmes, 1917–1935: some remarks on the Labour movement's contribution', *International Review of Social History*, xi, 1966.

73 McKibbin, R. 'The economic policy of the second Labour government 1929–1931', *Past and Present*, lxviii, 1975.

74 Marwick, A. 'Middle Opinion in the '30s: Planning, Progress and Political Appeasement', *English Historical Review*, lxxix, 1964.

75 Moggridge, D.E. *British Monetary Policy 1924–1931*, Cambridge University Press, 1972.

76 Nevin E. 'The origins of cheap money, 1931–1932', *Economica* n.s. xx, 1953, repr. in (77).

77 Pollard, S., ed. *The Gold Standard and Employment Policies between the Wars*, Methuen, 1970.

78 Sayers, R.S. 'The return to gold, 1925' in *Studies in the Industrial Revolution* ed. L.S. Pressnell, Athlone Press, 1960; repr. in (77).

79 Skidelsky, R. *Politicians and the Slump: the Labour government 1929–31*, Macmillan, 1967.

80 Stewart, M. *Keynes and After*, Penguin, 1967.

81 Winch, D. *Economics and Policy*, Hodder & Stoughton, 1969.

Bibliography

Primary sources

82 Amery, L.S. *The Forward View*, Bles, 1935.
83 Brailsford, H.N., Hobson, J.A., Creech Jones, A. and Wise, E.F. *The Living Wage*, ILP, 1926.
84 Craig, F.W.S. *British General Election Manifestos 1918–1966*, Political Reference Publications, 1970.
85 *Final Report of the Royal Commission on Unemployment Insurance*, Cmd 4185, 1932.
86 Hobson, J.A. *The Economics of Unemployment*, Allen & Unwin 1922, rev. edn, 1931.
87 Keynes, J.M. and Henderson, H. *Can Lloyd George do it?*, The Nation and Athenaeum, 1929.
88 Labour Party *How to Conquer Unemployment*, 1929.
89 Liberal Party *We Can Conquer Unemployment*, Cassell, 1929.
90 Macmillan, H. *The Middle Way*, Macmillan, 1938.
91 *Memoranda on Certain Proposals relating to Unemployment*, Cmd 3331, 1929.
92 *Report of the Committee on Finance and Industry* (Macmillan Committee), Cmd 3897, 1931.

BIOGRAPHIES AND MEMOIRS

93 Amery, L.S. *My Political Life*, vols 2 and 3, Hutchinson 1953, 1955.
94 Bullock, A. *The Life and Times of Ernest Bevin*, vol. 1, Heinemann, 1960.
95 Campbell, J. *Lloyd George The Goat in the Wilderness*, Cape, 1977.
96 Dalton, H. *The Fateful Years Memoirs 1931–1945*, Muller, 1957.
97 Feiling, K. *The Life of Neville Chamberlain*, Macmillan, 1946.
98 Greenwood, W. *There was a Time*, Cape, 1967.
99 Harris, J. *William Beveridge*, Oxford University Press, 1977.
100 Harrod, R. *The Life of John Maynard Keynes*, Macmillan, 1951.
101 Jones, T. *Whitehall Diary*, vols 1 and 2, Oxford University Press, 1969.
102 Macmillan, H. *Winds of Change 1914–1939*, Macmillan, 1966.
103 Marquand, D. *Ramsay MacDonald*, Cape, 1977.
104 Middlemas, K. and Barnes, J. *Baldwin*, Weidenfeld & Nicolson, 1969.
105 Pelling, H. *Winston Churchill*, Macmillan, 1974.
106 Rowland, P. *Lloyd George*, Barrie & Jenkins, 1975.
107 Skidelsky, R. *Oswald Mosley*, Macmillan, 1975.

108 Snowden, P. *An Autobiography*, vol. 2, Nicholson & Watson, 1934.

109 Taylor, A.J.P. *Beaverbrook*, Hamish Hamilton, 1972.

110 Young, G.M. *Stanley Baldwin*, Hart-Davis, 1952.

Index

117